PSYCHOANALYSIS AND ETHICS

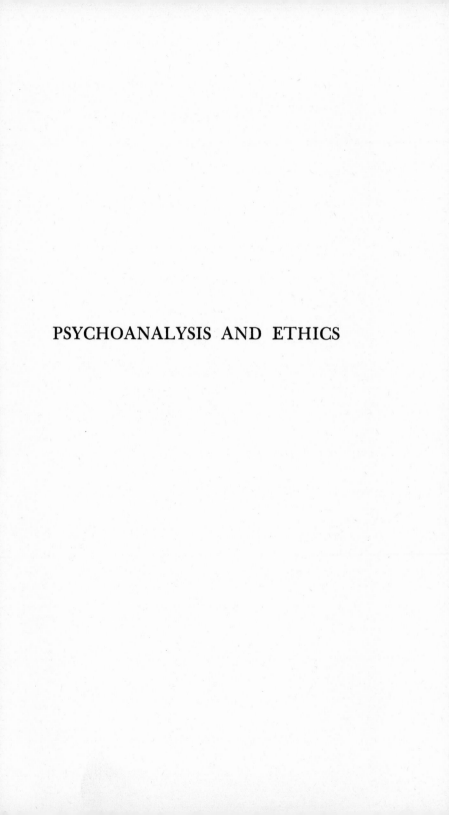

Publication Number 263
AMERICAN LECTURE SERIES

A Monograph in
The BANNERSTONE DIVISION *of*
AMERICAN LECTURES IN PHILOSOPHY

Edited by
MARVIN FARBER, Ph.D.
Department of Philosophy
University of Buffalo
Buffalo, New York

Psychoanalysis and Ethics

By

LEWIS SAMUEL FEUER

Department of Philosophy, University of Vermont
Burlington, Vermont

CHARLES C THOMAS · PUBLISHER

Springfield · Illinois · U.S.A.

CHARLES C THOMAS · PUBLISHER
BANNERSTONE HOUSE
301-327 East Lawrence Avenue, Springfield, Illinois, U.S.A.

Published simultaneously in the British Commonwealth of Nations by
BLACKWELL SCIENTIFIC PUBLICATIONS, LTD., OXFORD, ENGLAND

Published simultaneously in Canada by
THE RYERSON PRESS, TORONTO

Copyright 1955, by **CHARLES C THOMAS · PUBLISHER**

Library of Congress Catalog Card Number: 55-8858

Printed in the United States of America

CONTENTS

v

Contents

PSYCHOANALYSIS AND ETHICS

PART ONE

THE PSYCHOANALYTICAL FOUNDATION OF HUMAN VALUES

1. Does Psychoanalysis Lead to Ethical Nihilism?

ARE THE values of liberal civilization strengthened or undermined by the methods of psychoanalysis? Ethical nihilism is the consequence which many persons have drawn from Freud's ideas. They hold that social loyalties, under analytic scrutiny, dissolve into components such as the neurotic projections of guilt-feelings. Contemporary unreason envelops the psychoanalytical instrument; it argues that all values are irrational, that men's inner lives stand revealed in their nakedness as networks of senseless compulsions. The hero in Arthur Koestler's *Arrival and Departure* watches how his political values vanish, how analysis exposes "the false trails, demolishing meaningless catchwords like 'courage,' 'sacrifice,' or the 'just cause' " . . . "one had to discard from the beginning his so-called convictions and ethical beliefs. They were pretexts of the mind, phantoms of a more intimate reality . . . the real clue was this suspect craving for martyrdom." Koestler's hero had arrived at a stage of psychoanalytic nihilism—"the proud structure of his values had collapsed, and imperative exclamation marks had been bent into marks of interrogation." Does all ethical philosophy disintegrate under analysis like an unstable compound which breaks apart under intense light?

The ethical nihilist regards all social philosophies as systems of rationalization produced by such experiences as unconscious guilt. The values of the political radical

3

are reduced, for instance, to the status of disguised expressions of a revolt against parental authority. Psychoanalysis seems to banish sincerity from political relations. The political sceptic finds that it explains why the honesty of idealistic leaders is not to be trusted, and answers such questions, for example, as the aged Fabian asked: "Why did Mr. Ramsay MacDonald, after thirty years upbuilding of the British Labour Party, decide to do his best to smash it, . . . ?" The cold, shrewd answer which Sidney Webb gave leads to the psychoanalytical devaluation of political ideals. "The emerging leaders of the common people are neither pilloried nor bribed. As soon as they show evidence of political power, they are embraced!"[1] Ideals, from this standpoint, depart when their causal neuroses terminate. The direct satisfactions of power and place make superfluous the displacement of individual desires into social ideals. "Love of humanity" vanishes with high place because it was no more than the projection of one's own oppression, an overstatement which confounded humanity with one's self.

Political idealism, it is held, withers as unacknowledged selfish goals are achieved. When projective distortions are gone, humanity is perceived for what it is, with its crudity, pettiness, cruelty, stupidity. How ridiculous then to incorporate humanity into your basic scheme of values! Ethical nihilism seems then the logical culmination of self-understanding. "Love of humanity," it holds, is properly a neurosis which yields to therapy. An underlying nothingness pervades all values.

Psychoanalytical nihilism is an expression of the corrosion of universal, human values. It is itself the projection of despair. It issues from a betrayal of affections. The person who seeks to negate his affections, to deny them, and to mock at his self, declares that all values are null. Ethical nihilism is the consequence of a profound disturbance in men's social affectional life; the emptiness that it brings is like that of a rejected lover who tries to amputate within himself a whole segment of his emotions. Philosophers have always projected their loves and hatreds upon the nature of reality. They have tried to elevate to the highest reality that which they have prized, they have tried to deny the reality of that which they disliked. Realities thus corresponded to the hierarchy of one's values. And ethical nihilism is the projective negation of values which one would destroy, a suicidal attempt at one's own affections.

But the psychoanalysis which the ethical nihilist employs is, indeed, incomplete. For the distinction between rational and irrational values cannot be obliterated. In the hands of a master like Freud, psychoanalysis provides the basis for a valid critique of values which are irrational, inauthentic. It provides the instrument for clarifying the bases of choice so that men may perceive clearly their authentic values, the conditions for their happiness. It enables us to decide which of our choices are rational and which irrational. And authentic political values emerge, clarified and reinforced by the psychoanalytical critique. The "courage" perhaps which arises from unconscious fear and obedience to cruel authority dissolves, but the courage which is born from love is strengthened. "Values" which are predominantly modes of guilt-feeling, irrational edicts that issue from a childhood past, lose their hold, and are discarded as inauthentic. Rational values are confirmed.

What then are rational values? For the present we shall state the following. Rational values are those which diminish frustration and repression, the pains of cruelties and ambivalent feelings. Values are rational when they maximize the joys and satisfactions which are available under the given technological conditions. The task of social science is to help construct an order in which rational values are actualized throughout society.

Values are enjoyed likings, libidinal preferences, affections for objects and people. As the person grows from the childhood stage of self-love, narcissism, he develops a love for other persons and external objects. But the social environment often raises obstacles to the development of the social affections. Historically, the values which liberate men's energies have been born from movements of social reconstruction. The democratic sects of England in the seventeenth century, men like Jefferson in the American Revolution, were pioneers in a universal political ethics. A liberal social movement provides a source of values insofar as it provides the fulcrum for the substitution of affections for hatreds in our social system. It is a strategic direction for the remaking of the emotional configuration of society.

Ethical nihilism has lost sight of simple things. Men's anger at their treatment as unequals, their longing for a society in which their capacities for affection will not be stifled, in which they will not be tormented by anxieties of insecurity, all those motives which directed against repressive forces loom in history like a Great Quest, all this is omitted from the ideology of ethical nihilism.

For after psychoanalysis has unravelled the irrational components of inauthentic values, there still remains the rational foundation for authentic values—men's longing for joyful lives.

2. The Dilemma of Ethical Argument

Contemporary philosophers of the scientific school feel themselves, however, unable to provide the basis for a universal social philosophy. John Stuart Mill once said that "questions of ultimate ends are not amenable to direct proof,"[2] and Bertrand Russell speaks for the still prevalent view: "science cannot decide questions of value, that is because they cannot be intellectually decided at all, and lie outside the realm of truth and falsehood."[3] The scientific philosopher may invoke his own standards as an arbitrary final court of appeal, but he concedes that they have no warrant over other persons, or other cultures. Inductive social science seems to offer no basis for common values of mankind.

Then what is our alternative? If we forsake the method of empirical social science, what other method have we for arriving at a trans-cultural, ultimate, and universal ethics? Many philosophers have argued that there is a moral intuition which apprehends ethical truths valid for all men. But this attempted foundation crumbles under the classical criticism which John Locke made long ago. Locke showed that unconscious psychological pressures can masquerade as moral metaphysical intuitions. His analysis was the forerunner of Freud's search into origins. "Doctrines," said Locke, "that have been derived from no better original than the superstition of a nurse, or the authority of an old woman, may, by length of time and consent of neighbors, grow up to the dignity of principles in religion or morality. For such who are careful (as they call it) to principle children well (and few there be who have not a set of those principles for them which they believe in), instil into the unwary, and as yet unprejudiced understanding those doctrines they would have them retain and profess. These, being taught them as soon as they have any apprehension, come, by these means, to have the reputation of unquestionable, self-evident, and innate truths."[4] The moral faculty is too often the unconscious residue of our nursemaid's admonitions.

We seem then to be in a gloomy predicament. When we try to construct a social ethics upon an empirical basis, we seem led into descriptive ethical relativity, and can derive no universal, trans-cultural ethical ideas. The alternative direction leads us into metaphysical dogma, which cannot withstand psychological analysis. Science can then say nothing about ultimate values; but neither can metaphysics. What method is then available? What method of proof have we in ethical questions? At this juncture, the significance of psychoanalysis and the related social sciences begins to emerge. The conception of proof in ethics is transformed and validated. We may best show with examples the use of the psychoanalytical method in ethics.

3. The Psychoanalytical Verification of Ultimate Values

Imagine that we encounter a society of ascetics. They inform us that their ultimate value is suffering. We then criticize them from the standpoint of our own love for pleasure; we tell them how human experience is enriched when joy is the basic value. They reply to us indifferently that they don't accept our values. We seem then to be at an impasse. Presumably we may try to intimidate these ascetics or try through propaganda to have them repress their ultimate value. But evidently there is no common platform of scientific criticism.

This ethical dilemma is founded, however, on an assumption which has only to be stated in order for us to see how false it is. The assumption is that a person's verbal statement as to what his "ultimate values" are is an accurate report concerning himself. The ascetic who claims to value self-inflicted starvation and mutilation is taken to be an accurate reporter concerning his own psychical processes. But verbal reports are notorious for their untruthfulness, for their failure to penetrate to underlying levels of the personality. In reporting his values, the person is only too apt to state what he has been taught he ought to state. More important still is the fact that the "values" which are reported are those which are felt on the conscious level of experience. The conscious level has often repressed responses of evaluation which are more native to the person than the values to which he has given conscious acceptance. There have been questionnaires, for instance, which ask women whether they're happy in marriage. With high frequency, the women inform the interviewers that they are happily married. When more subtle methods such as apperception tests are used, they indicate much repressed discontent and aggressive impulse. The women conform to the code, nonetheless, of always appearing to be happily married, and indeed, they sincerely believe they are. But the truth of the verbal report must be confirmed with the psychological tools of inquiry which bring to view the more hidden layers of personality.

When the ascetic tells us, "I value my deprivation, I value my starvation," we might ask him to tell us his dreams and fantasies. We'll then find that his dreams depict with vivid symbolism a tremendous desire for food, and that they are filled with resentment against authorities who have pledged him to a life of deprivation. The deeper unconscious experiences of the ascetic are a rejection of the so-called values of the ascetic way of life. Simeon Stylites dreams of a soft, cool bed as he bakes on the pillar under the desert sun, Paphnutius longs for the voluptuous Thaïs, St. Jerome is tormented by the flesh.

People may overtly have accepted passivity as a norm of life, but their fantasies are then of self-assertion and a restored human pride. The Navajo dreams of a redeemer who will thrust out the white interloper,[5] the Jews through centuries of passive acquiescence dreamed of an all-powerful Messiah. No group in its deepest psyche makes "weakness" and "submission" into values; their fantasies are of strength and revolt. Beneath the level of the overt verbal report of one's "ultimate values," there is the testimony of dream and mythology, of behavior and tension, and this testimony cannot be unsaid by all the repressive devices which have silenced the inner questioning and doubt. Within the deeper levels of personality, the repressed, frustrated values of free choice lead an underground existence. There one finds the seething rebellion against superimposed "values," and alien "ultimate values" are in symbol destroyed. In these deeper levels of the self, there is the longing for another mode of life, though it be disguised in strange ways to state its protest in dream and fantasy. Within these deeper levels, we can verify the person's statements about his ultimate values. We can ascertain whether the total, underlying personality belies or confirms the person's conscious reports. An oppressed people, for instance, is often said to be "happy." So they tell tourists and travelers. Psychological analysis, however, tells another story. As John Dollard has written: "From the stereotype of the happy Negro no one can appreciate the actual amount of individual frustration and social turmoil which Negroes really endure."[6]

We can therefore enquire to what extent the "values" of a culture are repressive or expressive of its underlying, unconscious desires. The dreams of primitive peoples, for instance, enable us to measure the intensity of their allegiance to professed value-systems. As one anthropologist writes: "The evidence is strong . . . that dreams provide a 'safety-valve,' variously effective, which can contribute to mental health, or furnish a clue to the lack of it" . . .

"[they] frequently provide the only thread which can un-ravel the cultural cocoon in which the process of socialization binds all human beings, throwing into relief the unsocialized residue of the personality, as well as those areas where a culture has succeeded in applying the most effective control and support."[7]

Philosophers have tended to overestimate the truth-value of verbal pronouncements as to "ultimate values." That is why they have concluded that differences in ethics, like cultural disagreements, are irreducible, and beyond the province of science. But statements as to "ultimate values" are, as we have seen, testable. The whole ethical philosophy of Nietzsche, for example, is based on a psychological assumption that "a living thing seeks above all to *discharge* its strength—life itself is *Will to Power*."[8] Nietzsche's "ultimate value," the satisfaction of the will to power, presupposes a testable theory of human nature. Nietzsche assumes that the drive for power is basic and ineradicable in every human being. If this theory of human nature is confuted, the ethical doctrine, which is its expression, collapses with it. For statements about "ultimate values" are psychological assertions, and all the methods which are employed in psychological science can be used for their verification.

An assertion that a value is "ultimate" is, in effect, an affirmation that there is a corresponding unconditioned and irreducible drive in the human organism. The seat of ultimate values is the newborn child's primitive emotional responses. The infant responds with fear when it is deprived of support, or hears loud sounds, or is suddenly pushed. It catches its breath, cries. When we speak of security as a basic value, we are referring, in the last analysis, to such elemental facts of human nature. The infant whose movements are hampered responds with rage; the child whose arms are held tightly to its sides responds with crying, screaming, and striking. Freedom as a basic value arises from this groundwork of response. The infant who is rocked and caressed becomes peaceful; affection brings it contentment. And what one means by love as a basic value is rooted in such primal experience. The experiments of the child psychologist into what Watson called "the original and fundamental nature of man" are an inquiry into ultimate values.

When Nietzsche, on the other hand, says that "power" is an ultimate value, his assertion is not validated by the psychological facts of man. Power-seeking is not a primitive motivation; it is rather the outcome of experiences of a traumatic kind, deep disturbances of one's sense of security. From gnawing anxieties far within one's unconscious is born the exalted dedication to power. The shy, timid Nietzsche, rejected as a lover, dependent in his physical illness on his sister's care, would write her pathetically: "In the deeper sense I have no comrades—no one knows when I need comfort, encouragement, or a grip of the hand . . . And if I complain, the whole world thinks it has a right to wreak its petty sense of power upon me as a sufferer . . ."[9] And the same Nietzsche, friendless and insecure, would project his longings upon a cosmic scale; he would see the meaning of all existence in will to power, and in the guise of Zarathustra, his projective self, would admonish those who go to women not to forget their whip. The person who affirms power as his ultimate aim has failed to look deeply enough within himself. For when he enquires into the genesis of his "ultimate value," he perceives that it is not what he has basically wanted. The security and affection which were denied him are still sought with anxiety, and to overcome that anxiety, he wildly seeks power. Power, he believes, will bring him happiness, and appease the demon—anxiety within.

When a mode of behavior like power-seeking is elevated into an "ultimate value," when a goal is adopted by the person which is contrary to those primal to the living organism, when a means, valid in some situations, is turned into a universal end, two traits, typical of neurosis, come to characterize the person's experiences. Whatever satisfactions the person achieves, they will always be mixed with pain. The psychoanalyst Alexander once proposed as the criterion of neurosis "the principle that the neurotic psyche knows no satisfaction without suffering."[10] Because the source of insecurity is never removed, the inner pain never ceases; no matter how much power is garnered, the pain is not stilled, and its presence alloys the enjoyment. Secondly, there is what we might call a "non-terminating" property to false, neurotic values. The power-seeking person, for instance, is like an animal in an endless maze. No matter how much power he accumulates, his problem remains insoluble. The stimulus of anxiety always operates from concealment, and he is like a puppet manoeuvred by some force within himself which he cannot understand. The man who is driven by the anxiety of poverty to cumulate more and more money never knows terminal joys. He is caught up in an endless accumulation of means which never culminate in an experience joyous in itself. This regressive, non-terminating character of means without a goal, stamps the power-seeking experience with its anxiety-ridden source. An ultimate value of the personality is not one which is induced through anxiety.

The distinction between *authentic* values and *inauthentic* ones is one between values which are *expressive* of the primal drives of the organism and those which are *anxiety-induced*.[11] It is the contrast between values which are expressive of the free personality and those which are repressive through fear and taboo. This is the distinction which is at the basis of ethical theory, and the development of an applied social science for the working out of men's happiness.

4. Self-aggression in Cynicism and Pessimism

With the help of the psychoanalytical method, we can determine the extent to which different ethical theories express authentic or inauthentic values. An ethical philosophy is authentic when it affirms the individual's basic underlying values; it is inauthentic when it belies the individual's own deepest desires. We have an instrument for the scientific study of ethical theories, for we can examine them to see how their manifest assertions of value conform to the underlying realities of human personality. The task of ethical criticism is to bring the person to a more complete, honest self-understanding, so that the ethical philosophy he avows shall indeed be his own. Free choice replaces choice dictated by anxiety or fixation, which has paralyzed the will and disrupted judgment.

A knowledge of the historic settings to which ethical philosophies are responses is of great assistance in this work of criticism. We can then more readily ascertain whether so-called "ultimate values" are rather historically conditioned responses with a limited validity. For a response which is turned into an absolute imperative without reference to the highly special circumstances which may validate it, takes on the character of an inauthentic value-standpoint.

The ethical philosophy of the ancient Cynics, for instance, was a response to the troubled, uncertain social world, but it was likewise an inauthentic rendition of human values. "The Cynics," writes their historian, "were missionaries, and their message was that life could be lived on any terms the age could impose." The Cynics expressed "the desire to revert to a life based on the minimum of demands." They were the spokesmen of the subsistence level of existence. The Hellenistic world knew little security; exile was a normal political eventuality; slavery might befall the Greek traveller. "Exile, slavery, loss of home and possessions, are the frequent burthen of the Cynic diatribe, . . . they were performing a valuable service in showing that even these could be surmounted." The Cynics had undertaken to show that life at its worst was endurable. It was an age when hope for social reconstruction had collapsed, but, argued the Cynic, that was a matter of small import. Man could come to terms with any social realities . . . "their invective against wealth was as much for the spiritual benefit of the rich as for the material betterment of the poor."[12]

The denigration of human goods, the abnegation of joy and comfort, are however not ultimate human values. Rather they were attitudes which arose as responses to a social situation which made precarious the realization of human desires. When the social order frustrates the satisfaction of basic values, there is a mode of response which consists in "identifying" one's self with the world which deprives one of happiness. The cynic takes on the "tough" attitude, he mocks at himself and his own personality. All values become meaningless and hollow; there is a perverse pleasure in going forth willingly to deprivation, to self-denial.

I remember a troop ship which had sailed for many days along the Equator in the South Pacific. The stench from the sweating men, strapped in life preservers, was overwhelming. They had not bathed all during the voyage. They crowded the decks so that there was no unpeopled vacuum. The sun beat down upon them with remorseless indifference. The one open-pipe urinal was out of order, and, as the ship swayed its accumulated contents ran like a flood from one end to the other. Twice a day, the long queues would wind slowly into the ship's hold and come forth with tasteless food. A soldier beside me turned his bleary eyes from the sea, and said: "There are only three things that count: to fill your belly everyday, to empty your bowels in good shape, and to get your seven hours on the sack. That's all there is." His neighbors grunted in weary assent.

The cynical response indeed fails even to salvage what can be salvaged under the worst of conditions. The world of men may be in strife, and hatred may suffuse the land. Yet a man need not make himself the passive reflection of the social forces about him, hating himself and his values. For even when the soil grows harsh and unfriendly, one need not curse one's self too by laying waste to one's emotions. One need not make oneself a creature incapable of happiness. One can still say: This is not what we have chosen, and when we can, we shall choose another way.

Much that we have said of cynicism applies to the philosophy of pessimism. This doctrine, given its classic form by Schopenhauer, is under the stress of recent events, becoming once more widespread. That all human values are destined to defeat, that satisfactions are necessarily null, that vanity is the essence of existence, these are central tenets of pessimism. But even this conscious devaluation of human existence aims unconsciously to salvage what it can of the happiness of man. "In fact," says Schopenhauer, "the conviction that the world and man is something that had better not have been, is of a kind to fill us with indulgence toward one another . . . This may perhaps sound strange, but it is in keeping with the facts; it puts others in a right light; and it reminds us of that which is after all the most necessary thing in life—the tolerance, patience, regard and love of neighbor, of which every one stands in need, and which, therefore, every man owes to his fellow."[13] Beneath the pessimist negation of human satisfactions and values, one finds an underlying striving for affection and good-will among men. The subsequent effort of the pessimist to abrogate these strivings is a superimposed attitude; it is not the value standpoint which is original to the personality.

The pessimist outlook is inauthentic because it makes human defeat a self-willed enterprise. The social and physical environment frustrate our desires. Aggressive impulses against these obstacles well up within us. But the pessimist would re-direct these aggressive impulses against our persons and our values themselves. Schopenhauer does not advocate physical suicide, but he does, in effect, ask for what is an equivalent—the suicide of our values. He urges asceticism upon man, "a horror of the nature of which his own phenomenal existence is an expression . . . He therefore disowns this nature which appears in him, and is already expressed through his body . . . He denies the will and gives the lie to the body . . . Therefore every suffering coming to him from without through chance or the wickedness of others, is welcome to him . . ."[14] And this self-destruction of our values is not our own choice. It is rather an attempt to identify ourselves with the forces which oppose us, a resentment internalized within ourselves because it has failed to find its original object of action.

It is noteworthy that pessimism spread as a philosophy after the failure of the Revolution of 1848. Its historian has described it as largely a response to "the apparent failure of a social and political ideal which brought about this state of despondency." The oppressive militarist system in Germany, the suppression of free political movements, the crushing of social hopes, made men turn upon their own values. "To an outsider who has observed this half-smothered social disaffection, there naturally occurs the reflection that the pessimism of Germany has its half-hidden supports in these regions."[15] It was symbolic of pessimistic quiescence that Schopenhauer left most of his fortune to wounded soldiers and survivors of those slain in 1848 in defence of the Prussian monarchy against the socialist revolutionaries.[16]

Behind the pessimist standpoint on values and human happiness is the sense of defeat which has numbed the personality. There is a loss of the sense of reality of things, a loss consequent to the withdrawal of libidinal attachments from persons and things. A withdrawal of love can insure one against the sorrow of rejection. Reality then becomes pale and dull, a reflection of the partial death which the personality has visited upon itself. For the sense of reality is founded upon the person's genuine emotional concern for realities and their outcome. And this loss of sense of reality hovered around Schopenhauer's thinking. He had said: "He to whom men and all things have not at times appeared as mere phantoms or illusions has no capacity for philosophy."[17] The young Schopenhauer, who had stood in a Hamlet-like relation to his mother's lovers, had grown warped. His capacities for affection were uprooted with violence. He would draw comfort from the notion that love was a delusion, and he would try to sever his human longing for happiness. But the underlying repressed values and desire for affection asserted themselves in his summons to men to regard each other with the charity due to fellow-sufferers.

Pessimism is a defensive response for the mitigation of pain, but its response is inauthentic, because it tries to deny the values which are expressive of the underlying human organism. It is a defence mechanism which operates by reducing the human level of aspiration toward zero. It is a neurotic response because it has internalized aggressive impulses against one's self, and because it inflicts pain upon one's own person by destroying values and inhibiting the desire for affectionate relations. And the attitude of pessimism never achieves its sought-for equilibrium. For the self-directed infliction of pain is never satisfying, and the repressed desires for happiness are always surging within one's unconscious. The annihilation of life's impulses, the reverence for suffering, the internalization of defeat, are not values which the person has freely chosen. Pessimism, in this sense, is an inauthentic ethical standpoint.

It was significant that Schopenhauer turned for inspiration to the philosophy of Maya, that doctrine which was the response of the broken wills in India to the cruel severity of the caste system. This was the philosophy of those who, exhausted with life, wished to reduce all its experiences to illusion, and to have their individualities swallowed up in an encompassing One. Thus men offered themselves as willing sacrifices to a Totality; they destroyed their values and desires even as the Universe would otherwise do to them. This process of "identification" was the metaphysical enslavement of the social slave; it was not the free choice of an unbroken will.

When we recognize the source of pessimism, we see that it is not our value-standpoint. As human beings, there is a capacity for joy within us which we would keep alive. We then refuse to wipe out the last residue of our own individual feeling. It may be but a small fire in the night, but it is ours, a flicker of freedom which is valued even when annihilation overwhelms us.

5. The Psychoanalysis of "Good"

Confronted with the anxieties of men's decisions, what has been the response of American philosophy? We have seen that scientific philosophers like Russell simply said: science has nothing to say about ultimate values. And we have seen reason for believing this doctrine to be wrong. The great contribution of science is to help us determine which values are, indeed, ultimate, and to confirm, on the other hand, which are inauthentic, pseudo-values. What has American thought had to add to this problem? It is an index of American culture that the most influential recent essay on this subject makes ethics into a set of propagandist pronouncements, persuasive statements; the moralist is regarded as an effective technician in the instruments of emotive communication and manipulation.

The provocative writer on ethics, Charles Stevenson, enquires into the meaning of the statement "this is good." What does it signify? Its "analysis," he replies, is as follows: "this is good" is equivalent to "I approve of this: do so as well!"[18] What underlies Stevenson's analysis of "good"? Stevenson is an analyst of the American ethical language. What is his "good"? *It is the "good" which is the product of American salesmanship, propaganda, and advertising techniques.* These devices so permeate American culture that Veblen could characterize religion in America as the sale of "vendible imponderables."[19] Sociological science itself has been much concerned with the devices of successful persuasion. A recent volume by a distinguished social scientist is aptly called *Mass Persuasion: The Social Psychology of a War Bond Drive*. Propaganda, this author notes, is likely to expand in times of moral confusion. "When values are in flux, when competing parties and factions offer their distinctive ideological goods in the market place of opinion, when a unity of moral outlook has been suddenly shattered or has slowly decomposed into shapeless disagreements, the propagandist has his heyday."[20] The social scientist catalogues the thematic devices which achieve persuasion—appeal to the participative "we" feeling, to the pathos of familial emotion, to the call for personal succor, to the impulse of competitive emulation. Such techniques had been effective in selling thirty-nine million dollars of war bonds during one day's broadcast. Need we then be surprised when the philosophical analyst in American culture tells us that the meaning of "good" is its emotive persuasiveness?

Such an analysis of "good" sets forth what is largely peculiar to American cultural usage under the guise of a general analysis of ethical statements. Linguistic usages vary, however, in accordance with the dominant value-systems and emotional configurations of the different societies. There is no unique analysis of "good"; rather there are a multiplicity of analyses, or psychoanalyses, to be more exact. We can thus propose as a general principle: *corresponding to different social structures with their different personality-forms, there will likewise be diverse ethical languages, each with its specific psychoanalytical characterization.* What philosophers call the analysis of a given ethical language consists in effect of the first steps in the psychoanalysis of some particular cultural usage. And the latter will vary basically as we go from one society to another. We might provide a few brief samples of diverse cultural usages and their respective analyses:

(1) For an authoritarian state: this is good = I dislike this, but the State wants it; I fear the State, therefore I must repress my dislike, and say that I like it; and I shall find a channel for the aggressive impulses generated by my frustration by insisting that you should like it, too.

The meaning of "good" has a strong imperative vector in an authoritarian society. But in a liberal one it becomes less imperative in its significance, and more recommendatory.

(2) For a liberal society: this is good = I like this, and since we are so much alike, you probably would like it too.

This usage betokens friendliness; hatred components in its motivation are absent. "Good" has lost its demanding, compulsive, super-egotist flavor.

Calvinism was once defined as a system by which each exacts retribution from his children for the discipline inflicted by his parents.[21] A specific analysis of "good" corresponds to this cultural usage:

(3) For a Calvinist society: this is good = I dislike this, but was compelled by my father to accept it; now, having identified myself with him, whatever resentment I harbor against him will be deflected toward my own children, who will suffer as I did.

Within an order of ascetics, "good" reflects the dominant feeling of self-hatred.

(4) For an ascetic order: this is good = I dislike this, but my conscience hates me; therefore, I must endure it. But you need not endure it, because though my conscience hates myself, I do not find that it hates you.

A society's definition of "good" thus reflects its dominant underlying emotional configuration. Where aggressive impulses characterize the relations of men, their frustrations and hostilities will shape a conception of "good" which is removed from the simple likings of persons and things. "I like this" will then never be an antecedent clause in their definition of "good." What moulds ethical usages is the extent to which the users are dominated by hatred or affection. In general, we might say that two psychological coordinates must be specified in the analysis of the ethical language of any given society. First, we should know the quantity of affection or aggressive impulse which characterizes its cultural motivation, and secondly, we should ascertain the direction in which aggression or affection manifests itself, whether toward the self or toward others. Where, for instance, hatred pervades a society, the following is the exemplar of "good":

(5) For a society of diffused hatred: this is good = I dislike this, but was compelled by those I feared to accept it; now, filled with repressed aggression, I impose it upon others.

And, as a final illustration, we may return to the meaning of "good" as it emerges under the influence of mass media and mass persuasion:

(6) For a society of mass persuasion and propagandist techniques: this is good = your community, club, and set approve this, the best people approve this, desirable women approve this, the sound elements approve this, radicals disapprove this; I, whether I like it or not, "approve" this, therefore, do so as well.

We have thus rendered the meaning of "good" as it is used in different social situations. In a rigorous sense, however, we cannot say that we can define or analyze the meaning of "good." For in a strict sense, we might say that *ethical terms cannot be logically analyzed, they can only be psychoanalyzed.* Ethical language differs, in this respect, from scientific language. A scientific term for "force," for instance, can be defined as the "product of mass times acceleration." We can substitute one expression for the other in all contexts. But this is not the case with an ethical term. For example, let us suppose that we render "this is good" by "I approve of this: do so as well." It is evident that the latter expression will not induce the same emotions as the former.

What is distinctive of "good" in its usual ethical usage is that it evokes unconscious fears and anxieties; it ignites the sense of guilt. The penumbral responses to "good" reach deep into our unconscious. And the simple combination of a declarative with an imperative statement, "I approve this: do so as well," has none of this emotive unconscious, anxiety-inducing, guilt-evocative power. In this sense, no translation or linguistic device can pretend to be an adequate "analysis" of ethical terms. For the translation lacks that anxiety-inducing capacity which is distinctive of ethical language. Academic ethical theory acknowledges that "good" cannot be defined but only psychoanalyzed when it avers that it can only be "characterized," that it "bears the characteristic stamp of its emotional history."[22]

There is a most important consequence which follows from the fact that only psychoanalytical method can make explicit the anxiety-inducing property of ethical terms. It is this: *that the psychoanalysis of ethical terms tends to deprive them of their emotive efficacy as anxiety-inducers.* This was perceived a hundred years ago by John Stuart Mill when he wrote that "moral associations which are wholly of artificial creation, when intellectual culture goes on, yield by degrees to the dissolving force of analysis."[23] Analysis, he said, divests morals of their "sanctity." Mill's phrase, "the dissolving force of analysis," accurately describes what happens when the unconscious mechanism by which ethical terms ignite the sense of guilt is brought into full consciousness. The potency of these words as anxiety-inducers is diminished. To become aware of the unconscious sources through which these words exert their influence is to reduce their subterranean, magnetic tugging power.

Hortatory statements, or so-called persuasive definitions, for instance, lose their propagandist potency when they are subjected to psychological analysis. Take, for instance, such persuasive definitions as "good is holiness" or "good is obedience." Their purport is to influence attitudes by attaching to some behavior-trait all the emotive force of the super-ego's command. The super-ego, as Freud said, is "the representative of all moral restrictions," the residual power in our unconscious of parents, teacher, ministers, "the vehicle of tradition and of all the age-long values which have been handed down in this way from generation to generation." The super-ego has interiorized within the person commands which were, in origin, external. Words such as "good" are the language with which the super-ego speaks to us from our unconscious. But the analysis of persuasive definitions dissolves their persuasive power. When we understand how propagandist symbols are employed to sway our feelings, we tend to develop an immunity to their operations. Justice Holmes once advised those who would penetrate into the significance of ethical and legal concepts to wash them with cynical acid.[24] He observed how a notion like "duty" shrank when treated with this reagent. And it is the same with the notion of "good." Its influence upon us derives from the threats of some parent or nursemaid in our childhood; the word bears all the terror of a command in our earliest years when the withdrawal of affection was the ultimate sanction; it stirs up the now unconscious anxieties of our formative years. Clear insight into its functioning within us brings a liberation. We can then hope to revaluate our received values, and confirm their authenticity in terms of our own deepest desires. The false values, the inauthentic ones, tend to dissolve, as Mill said, under analysis.

Consequently, the ethics which has assimilated the standpoint of psychoanalysis diverges considerably from the "analysis" of academic ethical theory. The analysis of Stevenson, for instance, regards its labor as primarily a matter of sharpening tools. It has no wish to lay hands on ethical terms; it is prepared to retain traditional ethical

language with its rhetorical devices. "To point out persuasion," says Stevenson, "is not to condemn it." Our ideals
"must be fought for with the words 'right' and 'wrong'
else these attitude-molding weapons will be left to the
use of opponents."[25] If persuasive devices are the "tool of
the propagandist and soapbox orator," he continues, "they
are also the essential tool of every altruistic reformer the
world has ever known." Only by recognizing this fact,
shall we, it is averred, avoid the "passive or cynical neu-
trality" to which ethical analysis might otherwise lead.[26]

Academic ethical analysis usually employs an instrument which it refuses to follow to its final consequences.
The statements of Stevenson, for instance, which were
quoted in the preceding paragraph are not the consequences of his analysis. Rather they are themselves persuasive, propagandist statements, which reflect the special
social bias of their author. Bernard Shaw, a great soapbox
orator, caused something of an upheaval in English social
thinking when he forswore conceptions like "duty" from
his idiom. The gap between Shaw's language of human
realities and the ponderous phrases of his Oxonian contemporaries was immense. And in ethical analysis today,
we find the symptoms of a resistance-phenomenon in its
determination to adhere to traditional ethical terms. It
resists the fact that the whole consequence of analysis is
toward dissolving whatever usage is founded on anxiety-
inducing mechanism. The ethical analyst, like a psychoanalytic subject, resists the outcome of his own analysis.

The academic ethical analyst seeks to classify and clarify
the devices of ethical language. But analysis, it is believed,
need culminate in nothing more than clarity as to usage.
We have seen, however, that analysis cannot be impartial;
it cannot remain a spectator of usage; it alters the person's
susceptibility to anxiety-inducing ethical terms. We become aware that the language of public relations coun-

selors and lobbyists, for instance, is not unlike a bogus currency. Analysis cannot stop with classifying ethical language; it reconstructs it by bringing unconscious mechanisms into full view.

A basis for ethical theory emerges when we employ our analytic method with loyalty through to its conclusions. A basis for political philosophy emerges which is more reasoned than simple adherence to existent custom. Philosophy is more then than the classification of linguistic devices. The language of traditional ethics may dissolve, but a new conception of ethics, founded on the self-conscious strivings of human beings, evolves.[27]

6. Ethics as a Branch of Social Science: The Inquiry into Whether a Culture's Values Are Expressive or Repressive

When the dissolving force of analysis has done its work, the ethical language of anxiety-inducers tends to lose its functional basis in human activities. What conception of ethics arises to supplant that of the anxiety-inducers?

In a free society, it is our view that ethics comes to have the same relation to social science as medicine to biological science. There is then no distinctive ethical science with its unique, irreducible ethical terms, just as there is no separate science of medicine. Medicine applies all the biological sciences to help the patient in pain or danger. The patient comes to the physician with the hope that his distress will be alleviated; the physician, with his medical art, applies the relevant scientific information. Ethics is likewise the application of social science to human problems, human difficulties. People and societies are confused, anxious, hostility-ridden, tormented with guilt. The ethical thinker seeks the path for reducing anxieties, liberating affections, bringing men to clarity, diminishing the weight of guilt.

A conception of ethical theory arises in which the use of

anxiety-inducing terms has no part. It is one which is already found in practice among our most forthright social thinkers. Julian Huxley, for instance, has seen the beginning of a sound ethics in the liberation of the individual from primal guilt. Our morality, he has noted, has largely been founded on the mechanism of the super-ego, on the authoritarian attitudes of parents which the child introjects within itself. "This 'sphincter morality,'" he states, "is probably the first stage at which anything which can be called guilt is experienced."[28] The language of traditional philosophical ethics is, indeed, a rationalized precipitate of the authoritarian situations in which the child finds itself. And it is to be supplanted by an ethics of free men. As Lawrence K. Frank has written: "If such a proposed transformation appears to neglect the historically developed ideas and theories of social science and of ethics, such neglect is and always has been essential to any fundamental advance in knowledge."[29]

A suffering society is one whose values require analysis by the ethical philosopher and social scientist. The ethical philosopher tries to determine the extent to which its values are false, inauthentic, repressive. In Asia, for instance, ethical thinkers are finding that the so-called Eastern values are, in large part, inauthentic. They are trying to recover their own free choice of values. Soetan Sjahrir, later Prime Minister of Indonesia, during his confinement to a Dutch prison camp, once wrote on the problems of his people's freedom:

"But what is this Eastern spirit? It is, they say, the sense of the higher, of spirituality, of the eternal and religious, as opposed to the materialism of the West. I have heard this countless times, but it has never convinced me.

"Did not Hitler also say that the Aryan *Geist* was the sense of the higher, the spiritual, the moral, the religious?

And is this spirituality actually such a preeminently Eastern attribute and ideal? It seems to me definitely inaccu-
rate . . . the emphasis centers upon feudal culture with its
spiritualism and universalism." And what is this philosophy which is born of Asian feudalism? "The Eastern
philosophy of death is actually *the* Eastern philosophy,
and is not limited to Buddhism. The quality of nonexist-
ence as the highest ideal of life is a sort of general philosophy in this passive East. It is a mental attitude of disdain-
ing life, of turning from life, and thus of passively
accepting life and the world, without making any attempt
to change or oppose it. Consequently, there is the Eastern
concept that life *is* suffering; . . ."[30]

In these passages, an ethical philosopher is at work as
an applied social scientist, seeking to verify whether his
people's values are authentic. He enquires whether its
"values" are terms imposed by an order which makes
frustration the law of life. The ethical philosopher looks
for those modes of feeling and social organization which
will liberate men's energies: When Sjahrir sees the Eastern
art-forms as the bare rudiments of a feudal culture "that
cannot possibly provide a dynamic fulcrum for people of
the twentieth century," he is trying to liberate his countrymen from the distorted, inauthentic values embodied in
those art forms.

Such also is the method which Nehru has applied to
show the inauthentic character of Gandhi's ethics of asceticism. Gandhi preached the unlearning of modern tech-
nology and medicine. He advocated a return to the peasant's way of life. He drew his conclusions logically, and
said that any sexual act except for the sake of children is a
sin. Nehru replies by indicating how the false values of
asceticism arose from self-hatred and a conviction of guilt;
by bringing to full consciousness their origins, he deprives

them of their apparent sanctity. "Nor do I appreciate in the least," said Nehru, "the idealization of the simple peasant life . . . I want to drag out even the peasantry from it, not to urbanization, but to the spread of urban cultural facilities to rival areas . . . What is there in 'The Man with the Hoe' to idealize over? Crushed and exploited for innumerable generations, he is only little removed from the animals who keep him company." Gandhi, continued Nehru, was obsessed by the problem of sex. "For him it is a 'soot or whitewash' question; there are no intermediate shades."[31] Gandhi's autobiography indicates how his hatred for the human body was linked to traumatic guilt: "this shame of my carnal desire even at the critical hour of my father's death . . . is a blot I have never been able to efface or forget." Guilt-experience in the rebellion against a father can take traumatic forms, and the ethics of asceticism was begotten in self-punishment.[32]

The values of a free society are the expressions of an unthwarted emotional foundation. Potential feelings of affection are liberated from warping, constricting social forms. The creative imagination then conceives social relations in which emotional lives can grow to fulness, with minimal frustration and defeat. Happiness liberates human affections and energies through its own emotion, and all authentic values share in this liberation. As Sjahrir wrote in his solitude: "A consuming, deep emotion, a real happiness is never exclusive. One wishes to communicate it to others, and one becomes generous with it toward others. It is for this reason, I believe, that in the long run the highest personal happiness coincides with the general happiness and well-being of humanity. I believe, furthermore, that this is why pessimists, cynics, and egoists are really unhappy men—men who simply do not know how to make life yield the highest and fullest richness and beauty."[33]

The great ethical thinkers have indeed been men who pursued ethics as an applied social science. What was Spinoza's method, for instance, if not one of enabling men to reject inauthentic values, "inadequate ideas" he called them, and to replace them with "adequate ideas," authentic values?[34] Virtue, he said, "means nothing but acting according to the laws of our own nature"; virtuous action, as action founded upon the understanding of our own values, brings the greatest happiness.

"A man cannot be absolutely said to act in conformity with virtue, in so far as he is determined to any action because he has inadequate ideas, but only in so far as he is determined because he understands." Spinoza's faith in what psychological understanding would contribute to human freedom was such as to lead him to say that "a passion ceases to be a passion as soon as we form a clear and distinct idea."[35] Perhaps this is too extreme a standpoint, but it conveys the truth that the liberation from inauthentic values and false ethical doctrines begins with an understanding of their psychological sources.

The desire to live happily is, according to Spinoza, the very essence of man. Spinoza's ethical and political theories were an attempt to clarify the values of the free man which would contribute to happiness. The Calvinist clergy in the Holland of his time preached against pleasure, the theatre, and music. To them Spinoza replied: "It is the part of a wise man, I say, to refresh and invigorate himself with moderate and pleasant eating and drinking, with sweet scents and the beauty of green plants, with ornament, with music, with sports, with the theatre, and with all things of this kind which one man can enjoy without hurting another. For the human body is composed of a great number of parts of diverse nature, which constantly need new and varied nourishment . . ." To the Calvinist, brooding upon death and abasing himself before the Lord, he would say

that "humility is not a virtue," and that "a free man thinks
of nothing less than of death, and his wisdom is not a
meditation upon death but on life."[36] Spinoza spoke of
virtues and the desire of man; we speak of values and
underlying, biological needs and drives. The difference is
only terminological; the conception of ethics as the applied
social science of men's happiness is the same.

What is likewise valid in Nietzsche's ethical theory is his
psychological criticism of the false values of masochism,
the veneration of suffering for its own sake. What is
invalid in Nietzsche's theory is his own sadism, his inauthentic, "ultimate" value of cruelty. For Nietzsche's criticism of values did not penetrate to their depths. He did
not perceive that the false values of masochism are correl-
lative to those of sadism; there is no master-morality without a slave-morality. The free human ethics is one that is
without this inner antagonism. But Nietzsche did try to
found his ethics on a theory of human nature and on a
sociological analysis of moralities, and in so doing, he was
indeed regarding ethics as an applied social science.

Those who deny that ethics can be a branch of social
science declare that disagreements in attitude cannot be
resolved on scientific grounds. A person's attitudes, it is
said, can be reconstructed perhaps by emotive propaganda,
but they cannot be shown to be wrong. This emphasis on
the central status of "attitude" is typical of American culture, and it is natural that it occupies such an important
position in philosophic analysis.[37]

But an ethical theory which seeks to use all the resources
of the human sciences will not allow its vision to be re-
stricted by concepts largely moulded in propagandist
practice. Attitudes are not basic biological drives. Attitudes are often formed through dependence on pronouncements of adults. They are states of readiness, as Allport

has said, which are organized through experience, and which exert a directive influence upon the individual's response to situations. Attitudes thus rest upon a biological substratum of drives and needs, such as those for food, sexual satisfaction, security. And all that we have said concerning the verification, the authentication, of values applies as well to attitudes. Attitudes fixate social values, but any such scheme of values can be examined to see whether they arise from the individual's own free choice. We can ascertain whether a given set of attitudes contributes to the frustration or satisfaction of underlying biological desires. All attitudes are linked to the biological basis of human nature, but some are expressive whereas others are repressive.

Psychological inquiry enables one to retrace the path by which attitudes were acquired and to revaluate them; the individual is thereby enabled to re-choose his value-attitudes in terms of his own most basic emotional satisfaction.

Disagreements in attitude are not, to the ethical philosopher, ultimate lines of demarcation in human nature. Rather they challenge him to probe into the authenticity of values, to ascertain whether given attitudes are validated or invalidated by the person's own emotional choices. There are disagreements in attitude which may well be grounded in ultimate physiological difference; a person's preferences in foods may in large measure be related to the peculiarities of his physiological constitution. But these disagreements are indeed trivial; they are not the locus of those disagreements in value around which human controversies become intense. What is remarkable is the common pattern of value-attitudes which arises from the biological substratum, and which overcomes the most basic differences in metaphysical standpoint. The philosopher, G. E. Moore, for instance, may hold to an intuitionist metaphysics, but the things he holds most valuable are not different from those of more naturalistic men: the pleasures of human intercourse, the enjoyment of beautiful objects.[38]

The common values of life, the biological basis of man, provide the final criterion for the criticism of inauthentic values. A great moralist like Thorstein Veblen was thereby furnished with a powerful instrument for confirming the falseness of certain social values. Veblen noted, for instance, how the aesthetic taste of the leisure class was influenced by a requirement of conspicuous waste. "The canons of beauty must be circumvented by some contrivance which will give evidence of a reputably wasteful expenditure . . ."[39] The awareness of beauty of form is grounded in biological motivation and mode of perception; but this is not the ground of decorative showiness, which arises from a "value" for expensive display. Aesthetic criticism, from this standpoint, tries to arrive at what are genuinely our values, and enables people to discard spurious "values." The ethical philosopher clarifies the original, repressed underlying desires, which as long as the biological organism functions, cannot have been entirely obliterated by the enforcement through institutions of inauthentic values.

The psychoanalytical criticism of values is thus the primary work of the ethical philosopher. Freud's methods are a tremendous contribution to ethics as an applied social science. He provided the techniques for determining the extent to which attitudes are imposed or are the expression of autonomous choice, for the decision, in other words, as to whether values are authentic or inauthentic, expressive or repressive. As an example of such ethical criticism, we may cite Freud's discussion of "good" as used in the expres-

sion "good behavior." The problem concerned the decision
to educate children to attitudes of "good behavior." Freud
wrote: "I do not think there is even one good reason for
denying children the information which their thirst for
knowledge demands. To be sure, if it is the purpose of
education to stifle the child's power of independent
thought as early as possible, in order to produce that 'good
behavior' which is so highly prized, they cannot do better
than deceive children in sexual matters and intimidate
them by religious means. The stronger characters will, it
is true, withstand these influences; they will become rebels
against the authority of their parents and later against
every other form of authority." Freud thus criticizes a notion of "goodness" which is synonymous with the breaking
of the child's will. The same method underlies his analysis
of the ethics of sexual asceticism: "On the whole I have not
gained the impression that sexual abstinence helps to
shape energetic, self-reliant men of action, nor original
thinkers, bold pioneers and reformers; far more often it
produces 'good' weaklings who later become lost in the
crowd that tends to follow painfully the initiative of
strong characters."[40]

Freud's own basic values are not arbitrary; they are
rather what his psychoanalytical findings indicate to be
the underlying values and desires of all human individuals. Disagreement with Freud can only be significant if it
is likewise founded on factual grounds. But such disagreement would likewise be consistent with the conception of
ethics as an applied social science.

Formal philosophic analysis, on the other hand, tends to
lag behind actual practice in ethical science. As a formal
philosopher, Bertrand Russell, for instance, says that science has nothing to say about ultimate values. But Russell
has also written a notable essay, *The Harm that Good*

Men Do, in which he argues, for instance, that the rigid
rules of the Kantian moral law have a sadistic basis. He
asks for a return to Bentham's definition of a "good" man
as one who does good—"a man should be regarded as
'good' if he is happy, expansive, generous, and glad when
others are happy."[41] Whatever Russell may, as a formal
philosopher, say about values, here we have him, in practice, employing a conception of ethics as an applied social
science. We have him showing that the values of "good
men" are founded on restrictive taboos which are contrary
to their own deepest, underlying desires. We have him
applying a psychoanalytical criterion to the Kantian
ethic; he rejects that formalism as based on an inauthentic
value of cruelty. It remains to extend into philosophic
theory what already is done in ethical practice—to con-
ceive of ethics as the applied social science of men's happiness, as thereby competent to speak of "ultimate values."

Ethics, as an applied social science, has close relations
with politics, the science of men's governmental institutions. Academic ethics, however, preoccupied with linguistic devices, resists the suggestion that ethical inquiry
is related to great social issues. Stevenson, for instance,
avers that direct participation in practical reform "might
have its danger" for the analyst.[42] This makes as much
sense as a similar dissociation of the operational theory of
meaning from its application in the theory of relativity.
Philosophical analysis has been important precisely because of its direct, participative relevance to scientific
work. The great innovators and contributors to scientific
ethical philosophy were men like Mill, Spinoza, Bentham,
Adam Smith, who regarded their analyses as part of a
work of social reconstruction. Mill, for instance, undertook
his utilitarian analysis as an aid to his fellow philosophic
radicals in their struggle against the "ultimate" ethical

intuitions of English Conservatism. Ethical analysis, as part of an applied social science, is motivated by social interests. When John Stuart Mill sought for an epitaph for his departed master, Jeremy Bentham, he could think of nothing finer than to say "he is the great subversive of his age and country."[43] When ethics has ceased to be subversive, and has become content with the sight of unhappy men, its analysis has made a commitment which is not to freedom and science.

7. Resistances and Therapeutic Statements

Ethics, as an applied social science, is a branch of human knowledge. There have been thinkers like Plato who believed, furthermore, that knowledge would make all men good. "No man voluntarily pursues evil, or that which he thinks to be evil. To prefer evil to good is not in human nature"; a coward, for instance, is a man who is ignorant.[44] But the tragic fact is that men do pursue evil, that impulses of hatred overcome them, that knowledge can be powerless.

There are simple situations which preclude any undue confidence in "scientific ethics." Let us suppose that we are confronted with some Nietzschean or some masochist. We analyze his values laboriously; we show that they are not ultimate, that they are inauthentic; we exhibit the structure of his insecurities, the dynamics of his frustrations. After all this is over, let us suppose that our Nietzschean replies: "I have found your discussions very interesting. Nevertheless, I still propose to try to inflict as much pain upon people as I can." What are we then to do with our scientific ethics? We may have obtained the agreement of our Nietzschean to all our factual analyses, but at the end, he still chooses to act as he does. Has scientific ethics produced a common agreement on chosen action? Obviously not. Are we not then driven to rhetorical devices, propaganda, intimidation,—all sorts of extra-scientific ways of altering a man's choices? Why then pretend that scientific ethics is of avail?

We can probe into the lives of men dedicated to false values; we can bring to them knowledge and consciousness of their underlying motives. But after the knowledge is acquired, the evil is not always eradicated. The broken will is not repaired when the full story of how a child's impulses were stifled is told; the will to be cruel does not vanish when the narrative of frustrations is complete. Our social knowledge may be fragmentary, but it would suffice to build a much happier world. Then we ask: why will this knowledge not be applied? Why does knowledge fail to issue in action?

We are brought face-to-face with the most unPlatonic fact. Ethics as knowledge, as applied social science, may be inadequate when confronted with the facts of human *resistance*. There is an emotional determination in many persons to act in irrational ways, in ways contrary to their understanding. The warped wills, the broken wills, the power-hungry, the narcissistic, the sadistic, all have their resistances to the modification of their behavior. The broken will is too exhausted to try to act freely. The narcissistic person's capacity for affection and trust in human beings must be revived. The sources of human energy and affection can be like muscles atrophied with disuse. The children who came to Israel from Nazi camps would hide from others, and fear that each game might be a ruse to lure them to their death. They lived in fear, fear to undress, fear to take a bath, fear of adults, distrustful children who had lived in a world more cruel than Hobbes ever pictured his state of nature, a world where cruelty was endless and all-pervasive, so that the children's spirits withdrew like those of tired animals, who hope for their day's food, and long to be invisible. What message does knowledge bring to the broken will and smothered emotions?

Ethics as knowledge provides an insight into one's own values and a diagnosis of inauthentic choices. Sometimes this is enough to enable the person to mobilize his energies for effective, rational action. But this is not always the case; knowledge, confronted by strong resistances, will not succeed as therapy. This does not alter the character of ethics as scientific knowledge. There was an Aristotelian theologian who refused to look through Galileo's telescope. His emotional resistance to scientific evidence did not, however, affect the validity of Galileo's observations and theories. Similarly, emotive resistance to the propositions of ethics, as a social science, does not alter their scientific character. The social problem of human resistances remains, however, on our hands, and is itself a problem of ethics.

Freud has emphasized the fact of resistance, and distinguished it clearly from ignorance. "The idea that a neurotic is suffering from a sort of ignorance, and that if one removes this ignorance by telling him facts (about the causal connection of his illness with his life, about his experiences in childhood, and so on) he must recover, is an idea that has long been superseded, and one derived from superficial appearances. The pathological factor is not his ignorance in itself, but the root of this ignorance is his *inner resistances;* it was they that first called this ignorance into being, and they still maintain it now. In combating these resistances lies the task of therapy."[45]

The emotive resistances of neurotic cultures and persons to the analysis of their values and to the statement of the conditions of their happiness does not preclude us from affirming the propositions of ethics as a social science. What then shall we do concerning the resistances themselves? Our guiding principle is a truth of psychology: the emotive force of resistance must be overcome by another emotive force. As Spinoza said: "No affect can be restrained by the true knowledge of good and evil in so far as it is true, but only in so far as it is considered as an affect."[46] We are thus led to an important distinction in ethical theory, one which is of the greatest significance for an understanding of the role of ethics in human behavior. The distinction is that between *anxiety-inducing* statements, which we have already discussed, and what we shall call *therapeutic* propositions. What are therapeutic propositions?

Emotive resistances are the cardinal obstacle to the behavioral acceptance of authentic, happiness-giving values. How shall these resistances be overcome? How can a broken will, for instance, be strengthened? The great ethical teachers could give courage and self-respect to men. Their statements have always impressed the downtrodden: "The meek shall inherit the earth," "Ye are all equal—children of one Father," "The earth is the Lord's and the fulness thereof," "The Lord is my shepherd, I shall not want." These statements fulfill a therapeutic function. They strengthen the will of the person. They lighten the burden of his guilt. They assist him to look upon himself not as an object scorned but as worthy of love, a creature of dignity, an individuality which, whatever its station, is not to be despised. Translate a therapeutic proposition, and it says something like this: "We have faith in you, we like you. Do what you wish, discover your desires, we shall not condemn you." The person, aided by the affection of others, is enabled to cultivate the emotional resources which can overcome resistances; the autonomic system, with its reserves, comes to the assistance of the under-standing.

The embittered will, the shattered self, are the realities which therapeutic propositions help to reconstruct. The healthy, affectional elements of the personality have been famished and intimidated. They come to life with affection. The person's self-respect revives. That is why, for instance, a religion of love has brought hope to slaves, for the slave mentality is the outcome of a crushed will and is transformed by symbols of affection.

We might say that the function of therapeutic proposi-tions is to undo the damage which has been inflicted on the person through anxiety-inducing ethical statements. Anxiety-inducers inculcate certain attitudes and values through the use of fear. The man who uses such statements is trying to have you identify him with your super-ego, your conscience. Anxiety-inducers ferret out all the weak-nesses and guilt-feelings of the person, and make him all the weaker. For the burden of guilt becames the main-spring of action, not feelings of sympathy toward those to whom we are linked by affection, but guilt at disobedience to the super-ego. The vocabulary of ethics, as we have seen, has great powers for igniting tensions and anxieties; the experience of moral guilt itself is the result of a con-flict instigated between conscience and desire, between super-ego and ego.

Therapeutic propositions, on the contrary, lend support to the original and unextinguished free components of the personality. They counteract the resistances to free action which arise from the repressive forces of the social order. The internalized hatred and reproach which human consciences bear against their selves are mitigated, and affection comes in their place, with life-giving confidence. A god of love replaces the Calvinist god of hatred. The comradeship of a political party, with its own therapeutic language, can function in this respect as did the nonconformist sects in seventeenth century England. The taxicab driver in Clifford Odets' play of two decades back spoke for many like himself: "That's a new one for the kids—the reds is bogeymen! But the man who got me food in 1932, he called me Comrade! The one who picked me up where I bled—he called me Comrade too!"[47] Therapeutic statements liberate dormant energies; energies dissipated in self-hatred are re-directed into affectional channels.

Unhappy men dislike the savor of their own personalities. Their consciousness of themselves has become unpleasant. Forced to obedience, submissive to their superiors, hateful toward their inferiors, their characters have ceased to be their own. When asked what they desire, they don't know what to say. For the whole question seems absurd to them, as if somebody were mistaking them for a real person. And to such people, an ethical thinker offers real hope when he tells them: "Man is nothing else but what he makes of himself." Taken as a proposition of sociological science, this is clearly false. Everyone knows that traditions, upbringing, material conditions, have had an immense part in making us what we are. But take this proposition as a therapeutic one, and what does it say? It says: "no matter how you have been conditioned, frustrated, suppressed, there is within you some original feeling and desire which is yourself, which is not extinct so long as you have the energy to look for it within yourself; if it is kept alive and kindled, it will grow in force, till your revived self will break asunder the frustrational strata, bringing to your experience the freshness of new life. And we are confident that this you can do."

What is important in therapeutic propositions is not their manifest, overt content, not what they seem to affirm

as abstract truths. What is important is their latent, underlying significance. Therapeutic propositions convey to the
person the friendly emotions of others toward himself.
They are the vehicles by which the "social feelings of
mankind" secure expression in instances where a person's
life has suffered through insecurity and lack of affection.
They evoke the person's faith in his own capacities; they
call forth affections from people by giving them uncondi-
tional sympathy. Their significance is that the person
feels himself then within an emotional situation in which
affection predominates, and in which hatred, anxiety, and
insecurity can diminish. And resistances are overcome
through the healing support of the affection of others.
Ethics, as applied social science, becomes an operative
social force when its knowledge is guided by affection.
Ethical knowledge can be assimilated by people when
their wills have been strengthened by friendly feelings of
others which have reached into their unconscious.

The language of traditional philosophic ethics is composed, however, of anxiety-inducing terms. The vocabulary is the customary one of "ought," "duty," and "bad."
The ethical language of the toilet-training situation provides the model and archetype for much philosophical
analysis and speculation. We can therefore understand
why the modern effort for a liberal ethics began with an
assault on such notions as "duty." Bernard Shaw's *The
Quintessence of Ibsenism* was a landmark in this process
of ethical liberation. With a sense of the discovery of his
own freedom, he wrote, "Duty arises at first, a gloomy
tyranny, out of man's helplessness, his self-mistrust, in a
word, his abstract fear. He imposes that slavery fiercely on
his children, threatening them with hell, and punishing
them for their attempts to be happy." But "a sense at last
arises in him of his duty to himself. And when this sense

is fully grown, the tyranny of duty perishes; for now the man's God is his own humanity; and he, self-satisfied at last, ceases to be selfish. The evangelist of this last step must therefore preach the repudiation of duty."[48] Duty, for Shaw, was the primal curse from which we must redeem ourselves.

It is noteworthy that the ethical language of "duty," the terminology of anxiety-inducers, has been dominant in countries with authoritarian culture. The doctrine of Hegel, for instance, was one in which the individual will was led to identify its duty with the will of the all-inclusive State Absolute; this process was a metaphysical duplicate of that by which an individual renounces his will, to identify himself with the super-ego. An authoritarian family structure, moreover, adds its weight to the anxiety-inducers which express the social power of the authoritarian political form.[49] Anxiety-inducing terms were the emotional core of so-called idealistic ethics which exalted existent social forms and deprecated individual aspiration. "If a man is to know what is right," wrote Bradley, the Oxford philosopher, "he should have imbibed by precept, and still more by example, the spirit of his community, its general and special beliefs as to right and wrong . . . The person anxious to throw off the yoke of custom and develop his individuality in startling directions, passes as a rule into the common Philistine . . . There is nothing better than my station and its duties, nor anything higher or more truly beautiful. It holds and will hold its own against the worship of the 'individual,' whatever form that may take."[50] Anxiety-inducing statements thus contribute to the abnegation of the individual before the social order. The primal force of the super-ego speaks through one's station and its duties, and with unchallengeable ethical intuitions.

On the other hand, it is characteristic in democratic societies that the ethics of duty, of metaphysical compulsives, of anxiety-inducers, tends to vanish. The metaphysical ethics of Kant and Hegel is still to be found in academic seminaries, the stodgy survivors of cultural lag. But in a setting of friendliness, individuality, and equality, the anxiety-inducing ethics stands out as rigid, artificial, and cruel. Within a liberal society, there is a greater agreeableness towards each one seeking out that way of life which brings him the greatest happiness. Jefferson thus said of himself, "I too am an Epicurean," and wrote a syllabus of doctrines whch made happiness the aim of life. Furthermore, with an increase of goods, with the advent of an economy of abundance, the material groundwork exists for an attitude of good-will towards the diversity of individual tastes.

The Puritan ethic in pioneer America could claim the justification of necessity. Frugality and thrift were required to meet the challenges of scarcity, and the social system tries to make virtues out of necessities. When conditions of scarcity, however, were replaced by material affluence, the democratic society was prepared to receive the full criticism of the Puritan ethics. Ethical philosophers like Santayana then showed how Puritan values were what we have called "inauthentic": "To be a Calvinist philosophically is to feel a fierce pleasure in the existence of misery, especially of one's own, in that the misery seems to manifest the fact that the Absolute is irresponsible or infinite or holy."[51] The Puritan virtues were the means which helped people face the deprivations of pioneer life. But when these means were themselves turned into universal ends-in-themselves, into basic values, then an ethical philosophy of false values had arisen. And the method of demonstrating their falsity was that of the psychological and social analysis which we have already described.

In a society where affection predominates rather than hatred, the language of anxiety-inducers tends to become obsolete. Such a society is friendly toward the expression of individual desires; it is not predisposed toward their repression. The cruelty which lurks behind the anxiety-inducers is the kind of attitude toward children which Dickens depicted in *Great Expectations,* where Pip is brought up "by hand," Mrs. Gargery's hand, "hard and heavy," and where the local moralist, Mr. Hubble, pronounces children as "Naterally wicious." The ethical usages of anxiety-inducers are the counterpart of attitudes of hostility and repression in social relations. They decline in significance when there is no strong social motive for the control of people's behavior through mechanisms of anxiety, fear, and taboo. The measure of a society's happiness is in large part provided by the obsolescence of the language of anxiety-inducers, and its replacement by ethics, as an applied human science.

Where social relations, moreover, are characterized by stable affections and good will, there is a reduced need for therapeutic ethical propositions. Society, like a healthy patient, then no longer requires the reiterated assurances of emotional support. Its will is restored, and it knows its own values. Persistent recourse to therapeutic statements is evidence of a failure of will. There are persons whose illnesses have proved insuperable to the resources of psychotherapy. There are persons whose wills have been so destroyed that only emotional sustenance of the most extreme sort enables them to survive.

8. Modes of Identification: Repressive and Liberational

Ethics, as the applied social science of men's happiness, can only flourish in a society where the "social feelings of mankind" (in Mill's phrase) are well developed. The sympathies, the affections, the social feelings of men involve an experience of identification with others which is the ultimate source of ethical action. But there is another mode of "identification" which generates cruel behavior; the two kinds of "identification" experience must therefore be distinguished.

The experience of affectional identity is, of course, found at its highest in the experience of intense love. Emily Brontë in her novel *Wuthering Heights* describes the feeling of complete identity which Catherine had for Heathcliff: . . . "he's more myself than I am. Whatever our souls are made of, his and mine are the same . . . My great miseries in this world have been Heathcliff's miseries, and I watched and felt from the beginning; my great thought in living is himself. If all else perished, and he remained, I should still continue to be; and if all else remained, and he were annihilated, the universe would turn to a mighty stranger: I should not seem part of it . . . I am Heathcliff! He's always, always in my mind: not as a pleasure, any more than I am always a pleasure to myself, but as my own being."

Affectional identification, at its highest, heightens and intensifies the energies of the lover. It is life at its fullest; in its lesser forms, in the various degrees of sympathy, it constitutes the "social feelings of mankind," the one secure emotional foundation for ethical action. A durable world order of peace depends, in the long run, on the achievement of a diffused affectional identity among all the races and peoples of mankind, a sufficient bond of common sympathy whose natural expression is cooperative behavior.

But there is another sense of "identification" which arises not from affection but from fear. When men, for instance, "identify" themselves with their masters, they suppress what are genuinely their own personalities; they abdicate their own will with weariness to enthrone within themselves the will of another. Exhaustion weakens the sense of one's own will. The power of a child, for instance, can be broken; the child's will, in tired surrender, takes on a vassal's relationship to some dominant authority. This is what Freud calls an "identification," "that is to say, that one ego becomes like another, one which results in the first ego behaving itself in certain respects in the same way as the second; it imitates it, and as it were takes it into itself." As people grow older, they forget the difficulties of their own childhood, "and are glad to be able to identify themselves fully at last with their own parents, who in their day subjected them to such severe restraints." The mechanism of identification herein is one in which the ego links itself to what Freud calls the super-ego. The latter is the psychological formation, largely unconscious, of the moral training of our childhood. It remains with us in later life, "the representative of all moral restrictions, the advocate of the impulse toward perfection, . . . the vehicle of tradition of all the age-long values which have been handed down in this way from generation to generation."[52] The identification with the super-ego, we might add, is one which is anxiety-induced. It is the outcome of submission to fear.

"Identification" with the super-ego is not a liberational experience; it is repressive. It represents the subdual of your own character, a capitulation of your desires to a stronger external force. Henceforth, the personality has within it an element of cruelty directed against itself. The cruelty of society, the state, the family, is internalized within oneself, and transmuted into a self-willed cruelty. The reasoning of idealistic metaphysics often tries to portray this "identification" as philosophically necessary. Bradley, for instance, says that the individual apart from the community is an abstraction, that his individuality is like a predicate of the community; and a predicate can't exist apart from the subject. This linguistic analogy has no bearing on the problems of men's relations. Robinson Crusoe is quite real, though he lives alone. The richness of a man's experience may depend, in part, on his social relations, but his reality is not adjectival to some subject (community) which exists over and above him. Our social relations are concrete social facts; they do not make us metaphysical predicates. The notion that we become "real" only through "identification" with a reality higher than ourselves must be regarded as a formula designed to secure our consent to a denial of self which otherwise arouses the rebellion of our deepest desires.

The social affections, the social feelings of mankind, provide the only mode of identification which is liberational. Unlike the super-ego, social feelings are not an amalgam of sadistic and masochistic components. Affections entail a direct pleasure in the society and existence of others; they involve an absence of the anxiety of latent hostility; they bring a sense of security in which one's own values grow in free expression. A society where affectional identities are dominant naturally approaches its social problems with the purpose of solving them in terms of human happiness. Ethics is then conceived as an applied human science. Repressive "identifications," on the other hand, are the psychological mechanism of anxiety-inducing traditional ethical terms. They are obsolescent in a free society where the social feelings of mankind have been allowed their maximal growth.

9. Utilitarianism Rewritten

The ethical theory which we have been proposing is, as has been evident, in the tradition of the liberal utilitarianism of John Stuart Mill. But Mill's philosophy has often been severely criticized, and is generally regarded as an inadequate foundation for ethical philosophy. In what way then does our own analysis differ from Mill's theory, and how do these points of difference make it possible to provide a secure basis for liberal ethical theory?

The difficulties which beset Mill's utilitarianism vanish when it is placed upon a sound psychological foundation. Mill tried to bridge the psychological gaps in his theory with tenuous logical constructions. The liberal ethics, however, has its natural basis in psychoanalytical theory; it then becomes authentic and self-consistent.

The Principle of Utility, or the Greatest Happiness Principle, which Mill proposed, holds that "actions are right in preportion as they tend to promote happiness, wrong as they tend to produce the reverse of happiness."[53] In Benthams's form, it was the principle that an action is good if it promotes the greatest happiness of the greatest number. Mill tried to prove this principle with three arguments, each of which is independent of the others. Only one of them is cogent. We shall call the first argument of Mill the logical, the second, the appeal to conscience, and the third, the social feelings of mankind.

Mill's logical argument for the Principle of Utility is the following: each person, he says, desires his own happiness; hence, it follows that since each person's happiness is a good to that person, that therefore the general happiness is a good to the aggregate of all persons. That this argument is unconvincing can be seen if we were to propose as a basis for an alternative ethics a Principle of Disutility. In other words, let us imagine that we affirm our natures to be such that we take delight in the suffering of others. Then the condition for my happiness as an individual would be the Greatest Misery of the greatest Number. Something akin to such a Greatest Misery principle underlies the ethics of Nietzsche. The general happiness would then be an evil as far as I am concerned. There is no bridge which can be constructed out of pure logic from the desire for individual happiness to that for the general happiness. If such a bridge exists, it must be fashioned from the psychological materials of the human affections.

Mill's second argument for the Principle of Utility consists of a reference to what he calls "the ultimate sanction of all morality," namely, "the conscientious feelings of mankind." The essence of conscience, says Mill, is the pain which is attendant on the violation of duty. And Mill believes that such pain is the consequence of acts which are against the happiness of the greatest number. But there is a genuine difficulty in this effort to base the principle of utility upon the human conscience. For as Mill says specifically, the moral feelings are not innate but acquired. The child is not born with a sense of guilt. The moral faculty, Mill states, can by "the force of early impressions" be cultivated in almost any direction so that almost any institution or practice can be endowed with "the authority of conscience." The mystical character which surrounds the idea of moral obligation arises, according to Mill, from the complicated psychological origins of conscience. Conscience, says Mill, is "all encrusted over with collateral associations, derived from sympathy, from love, and still more from fear; from all the forms of religious feeling; from the recollections of childhood and of all our past life; from self-esteem, desire of the esteem of others, and occasionally even self-abasement." This analysis of conscience is almost identical with that of Freud.

We have already seen that psychological analysis undermines the unconscious emotive powers of ethical language. We have referred likewise to Mill's view that "moral associations which are wholly of artificial creation, when

intellectual culture goes on, yield by degrees to the dissolving force of analysis." Will conscience, which is also
of artificial creation, withstand an analysis into its origins?
The dissolving force is at work when childhood fears
which are the source of guilt-feelings are brought from
the unconscious into consciousness. Analysis is like a light-
spectrum which disintegrates the molecular bonds of the
unconscious, and allows the liberated components to come
to the surface. The mysterious monarch of our conduct
turns out to have plebeian origins. We cannot base the
principle of utility upon moral associations which may be
dissolved by self-knowledge.

We are thus brought to the final argument for the
Greatest Happiness principle, one which takes us indeed
to the psychological nature of man. What the dissolving
force of analysis does not eliminate is the ultimate residue
which is the "natural basis of sentiment for utilitarian
morality." "This firm foundation is that of the social feelings of mankind; the desire to be in unity with our fellow
creatures which is already a powerful principle in human
nature, and happily one of those which tend to become
stronger, even without express inculcation, from the influences of advancing civilization." Mill recognizes the
ambivalences in our feelings toward others which are so
characteristic of our civilization. "This feeling in most
individuals is much inferior in strength to their selfish
feelings"; nevertheless, this social feeling "is the ultimate
sanction of the greatest happiness morality."[54]

Man's affective nature is the basis for liberal ethics—
man's affection and sympathy for others, and the feeling
that their joys are his and their sorrows likewise, a feeling
of jointness with others. But now the crucial problem for
this psychological basis of ethical life faces us. These feelings of unity with others which Mill describes are only

too often lacking. Selfishness, separateness, alienation, division, egoism, are widespread traits of the human character. How prim and ridiculous then does the utilitarian ethic begin to sound. Disraeli, the political realist, saw Mill rise to address Parliament; he remarked with sarcasm: "Ah! I see! the finishing governess."[55] Are the social feelings of mankind the delicate construction of a fastidious mind which would exclude the hatreds which fester among men from its orderly arrangement of the social furniture? Mill himself acknowledged that there are individuals in whom social feelings seem altogether wanting, men who are selfish, and concerned only with their own happiness, not that of others. If so, are we not back to a doctrine of individual hedonism? And is not this hedonism of a kind which may be consistent with a total lack of concern for social well-being?

The egoist hedonist is a person, however, who has limited his capacity for happiness. The egoist has affection for no person other than himself; he is what is called in psychoanalytic theory a narcissist. But egoism, narcissism, represent a withdrawal of the libidinal, affectional energies; they are constricted within the self's narrowest dam. Where the self is the sole object of affection, there is an incapacity to extend one's libidinal interests or values to other persons, objects, and activities. There is, moreover, a feeling of anxiety and apprehension that others are a threat to one's self. The selfish person is an unhappy person; all the joy-giving avenues of affection and delight in others are closed to him. A sickness is within him that has prevented his affections from growing out from within himself. The narcissism, the selfishness, of the sick is described by Freud:

"It is universally known that a person suffering organic pain and discomfort relinquishes his interest in the things of the outside world, in so far as they do not concern his suffering. Closer observation teaches us that at the same time he withdraws his libidinal interest from his objects: so long as he suffers, he ceases to love . . . the sick man withdraws his libidinal cathexes back upon his own ego, and sends them forth again when he recovers . . . The familiar egoism of the sick person . . . so natural because we are certain that in the same situation we should behave in just the same way."[56]

The person whose emotional concern has narrowed down to his "self" in the sense in which "self" signifies an absence of affections or interests in other persons and things does not derive the maximal happiness or satisfaction of which his life's energies were capable. The unhappiness of the narcissistic sick person has an internalized source. The person who always acts hatefully is distorted from within by some source of pain and resentment toward others. Narcissism, from this standpoint, is an inauthentic, false value. It was imposed on the person from without, by illness or lack of affection. It was not a value chosen in the fulness of emotional satisfaction. In his unhappiness, the narcissist affirms himself an egoist, as concerned only with his own welfare. Bad news about people he knows may momentarily please him, but the illness remains, unappeased and ever obtrusive, so that his unhappiness is always with him, knowing only the temporary anodyne of the unhappiness of others.

The happiness of the self and the happiness of others are emotionally indissoluble. Only if one's own social feelings are developed will one know all the happiness of one's own inner life. The happy man takes joy in the happiness of others. The greatest happiness of others is part of the fulfillment of his own. This is the foundation of the liberal ethics. The desire to work for the happiness of others then arises from one's own affectional life. It is not the dictate of an anxiety-inducing imperative. How significant this distinction is for the liberal ethics can be seen from a brief study of the psychological history of John Stuart Mill himself.

10. The Crisis of John Stuart Mill: A Case Study in the Psychoanalysis of Ethics

The famous crisis in Mill's life brought to the fore all the essential problems in the ethics of human happiness. Mill was twenty years old, "in a dull state of nerves . . . unsusceptible to enjoyment or pleasurable excitement," when he asked himself the following question:

"Suppose that all your objects in life were realized; that all the changes in institutions and opinions which you are looking forward to, could be completely effected at this very instant: would this be a great joy and happiness to you? And an irrepressible self-consciousness distinctly answered, 'No!' At this my heart sank within me: the whole foundation on which my life was constructed fell down . . . I seemed to have nothing left to live for."[57]

There were, furthermore, symptoms of deep anxiety in Mill. He was "seriously tormented by the thought of the exhaustibility of musical combinations." He reasoned that the finite tones of the octave could be combined in only a finite number of beautiful ways, and that the possibilities of musical creativity would become exhausted. "This source of anxiety may perhaps, be thought to resemble that of the philosophers of Laputa, who feared lest the sun should be burnt out." Mill was also worried by the thought that happiness itself might become extinct in a perfect social world: "if the reformers of society and government could succeed in their objects, and every person in the community were free and in a state of physical comfort, the pleasures of life, being no longer kept up by struggle and privation, would cease to be pleasures."[58] Social reform, Mill feared, would put an end to the very happiness which it sought.

More than a half year elapsed before Mill surmounted this extreme dejection. He was reading Marmontel's *Mémoires* one day, "and came to the passage which relates his father's death, the distressed position of the family, and the sudden inspiration by which he, then a mere boy, felt and made them feel that he would be everything to them— would supply the place of all that they had lost. A vivid conception of the scene and its feelings came over me, and I was moved to tears. From this moment my burden grew lighter. The oppression of the thought that all feeling was dead within me, was gone." Wordsworth's poetry also gave him "a source of inward joy, of sympathetic and imaginative pleasure, which could be shared in by all human beings; which had no connexion with struggle or imperfection, but would be made richer by every improvement in the physical or social condition of mankind."[59]

It is a remarkable psychological fact that relief came to Mill upon reading of the death of a father. It restored to Mill his own capacity for feelings, and we may surmise that the passage conveyed to him a symbolic depiction of his own father's death. James Mill, the father, had crushed his son's capacities for feeling, and had turned him into "a mere reasoning machine"; James Mill was the "last person" to whom the son, in his crisis, would turn for help; he was a father who lacked tenderness toward his children so that they feared him. Sadly John Stuart Mill avowed that he could not honestly say he loved his father, he was "loyally devoted to him."[60]

Mill had been brought up with a strict emphasis on his *duty* to work for the happiness of the greatest number.

His father inculcated this principle with all the force of parental authority. But the child whose own need for affection has not been satisfied will grow up lacking spontaneous social feelings and affection for others. The child whose affectional need is frustrated will tend to have a dislike, suspicion, or anxiety with respect to others; there will be a general diffidence in his character. The ethical imperative, the anxiety-inducing duty to work for the happiness of others is not then something which can withstand analysis. When it collapses, there is no emotional affective basis on which one's social activities will rest. And the young Mill saw indeed that his utilitarian activities were in conformity with an anxiety-inducing imperative; he found no happiness within himself when others were happy. Thus he fell into a complete dejection, which did not leave him till the symbolic death of his father opened within him the possibilities of free emotional expression; then he found that normal social affections and feelings could finally grow inside himself. The restraining anxiety of the parental symbol was gone.

The only durable basis for the ethics of happiness is the person's own happiness, his joy in his activities and affections for others. Where social activities are induced solely through the pressure of duty or conscience, the various phenomena of anxiety and guilt ensue—personal dejection, masochism, or a violent rebellion against parental authority, with consequent selfishness. Through his crisis, Mill learned that the cultivation of emotional experience and social affections was essential for the structure of his liberal ethics. . . . "I, for the first time, gave its proper place, among the prime necessities of human well-being, to the internal culture of the individual. I ceased to attach almost exclusive importance to the ordering of outward circumstances, and the training of the human being for speculation and for action. . . . The cultivation of the feelings became one of the cardinal points in my ethical and philosophical creed."[61]

Social feelings are not cultivated by precepts of duty, anxiety-inducing terms, or ethical imperatives. The commandment to honor one's parents will not make one love them. Love for others is born primarily from the experience of having been loved and respected in one's early years. And in this sense, the cultivation of the feelings is something which is done by the whole social environment of the person. The social feelings grow in a setting of affection, and it was this which was denied to Mill in his formative years. Mill's "devotion to mankind" in his youth was an abstract matter, a well-done recital of lines that he had been compelled to memorize by his father. The emotional basis for his political activities was without conviction. This was the reason for the tremendous impact of the question which Mill asked himself. He would not be happy if all those for whom he worked were happy. Why? Because he loved no one, and felt his capacities for affection depleted. His education had come near making him incapable of loving any one. There is a character in Joseph Conrad's novel *Victory* who has likewise been taught by his father to mistrust life; his tragedy is his inability to meet the love of another person, and he finally calls woe to the man whose heart has not learned while young to hope and to love. Mill's own experience was more fortunate. His love for Mrs. Taylor during later years basically affected his personality. Mill had the resources within himself to maintain this love despite the disapproval of his father and friends, and it gave to his subsequent political work a character of power and sincerity which it had previously lacked.

Mill feared that pleasures which would be come by

without social privation would lose their character as pleasures. This we might call the "reformer's fallacy," for it is peculiarly associated with components in the reformer's motivation. Although social affections guide the reformer, there is often within him also a strong ingredient of aggressive impulse. He then takes pleasure in his struggle against evil, not just because it's evil he's against, but because he enjoys a struggle, he enjoys a fight. This ingredient of aggressive impulse expresses itself in the demand that every joy be preceded by privation, the opportunity, that is, for a struggle. But this demand is itself the symptom of an inner disturbance, which has made a false ultimate value out of struggle. The repressed aggressive feelings which Mill bore towards his father evidently made it seem that every genuine pleasure must necessarily be the outcome of painful struggle. It was evidently Mrs. Taylor's influence which gave to his reforming impulses a more humane basis in social affections. We can understand then why Mill would speak of her as one who had saved him from an unending bleakness.

From his crisis-experience, Mill learned, moreover, that happiness cannot be taken as a narcissistic concept; happiness involves not an absorption with oneself but an emotional interest in objects and persons outside what is otherwise a narrow ego. "I now thought that this end was only to be attained by not making it the direct end. Those only are happy (I thought) who have their minds fixed on some object other than their own happiness; on the happiness of others, on the improvement of mankind, even on some art or pursuit, followed not as a means, but as itself an ideal end. Aiming thus at something else, they find happiness by the way . . ."[62] Happiness itself, in other words, is not a person or an object; it is the quality of a person's psychophysical experience when the latter is constituted of satisfactions in affective interests in persons, things, activities. Critics like Bradley have charged that Mill was abandoning the happiness ethics when he advised people not to take happiness as the conscious end. But this is no different from the practice of the physician who advises his patient to enjoy his work, games, and food, or who seeks to restore the capacities for such enjoyment; to be preoccupied with health, as an end always before one's mind, would be a symptom of hypochondria. Every joyful experience is one of joy in some person or object; it is not the experience of joy in abstract isolation. Activities directed by affections for persons and things constitute happiness, for happiness is the satisfaction of libidinal interests.

The unhappy person is one whose experience is painful, dull, or uninteresting. It would be of little avail to tell him to seek happiness. What he requires is a diagnosis which will explain why his activities are not happiness-giving, why his experiences are neutral and gray, lacking in the joy component. Happiness as the fulfillment of our affections and activities is not separable from them. In this sense, one must forget one's self to attain happiness, and give one's self to the activities which are expressive of our values. Mill's love of mankind was, in his youth, something thin, which wore itself out; it could survive only if it was the outcome of feelings of affection which overflow into social activities. And this, Mill, the young reasoning machine, had not yet experienced.

Whether Mill ever completely overcame the effects of his education is, of course, questionable. The question, "are you happy?" was one which he was still inclined to repress. "Ask yourself whether you are happy," he wrote, "and you cease to be so."[63] But this question would ruffle only the person who wishes to repress some inner doubt as to his happiness. The question brings into clear consciousness the judgment of one's life, and would not disturb the happy person. If the question disturbs, then the source of the disturbance is not removed by its repression.

It remains true that what was lacking in the utilitarian writers was a sense of the rich experience of joy. The utilitarians had accepted happiness as the aim of life; they wrote political pamphlets on this assumption, and conducted a great social movement. But a dour Calvinist asceticism largely controlled their unconscious thoughts and feelings. The Scottish Presbyterian upbringing always ruled the living habits of James Mill. His son wrote of him: "For passionate emotions of all sorts, and for everything which has been said or written in exaltation of them, he professed the greatest contempt. The 'intense' was with him a by-word of scornful disapprobation."[64] A philosopher of this stamp can write much about pleasure and hedonism, but his words convey only a small part of himself; the verbalized doctrine is inconsonant with the man's total experience. As a thinker, James Mill translated the Calvinist ethics into a utilitarian terminology; it was a change in language-form, but the underlying emotional spirit was unaltered.[65]

The sense likewise that free, spontaneous joy is essential to happiness was lacking to Jeremy Bentham. He could therefore forget that happiness, without liberty, is impossible. Bentham, the organizer of people's lives, could thus become the precursor of bureaucratic ethics, as when he wrote: "Call them soldiers, call them monks, call them machines, so they were but happy ones, I should not care. Wars and storms are best to read of, but peace and calms are better to endure."[66] Men cannot be conceived of as soldiers, monks, or machines without the corollary of the proposed frustration of large segments of their instinctual

lives. Yet Bentham could envisage happiness as arising in
entities that were mechanically responsive and emotionally impoverished. Free choice had vanished from his system. There is a sort of "happiness" in the anchorite's cell
and in the soldier's barracks, a kind of substitute product.
It is the "happiness" of a negative adjustment, the cultivation of insensitivity to one's surroundings, a low-level
equilibrium which involves no aspiration to intense experience. This is not the happiness of the liberal utilitarian;
it is the false, inauthentic value of the bureaucratic utilitarian, an imposed "happiness" which the human personality rejects. The bureaucratic utilitarian would speak in
Bentham's pronouncements. "I shall be the dead legisla-
tive of British India. Twenty years after I am dead, I
shall be a despot."[67] The choice of words, of "despot," por-
tends what happens to the utilitarian ethics when it for-
gets that freedom is a constituent of happiness. The
"scientific ethics" of a bureaucratic group can then solve
many problems, but not that of human happiness.

11. The Limits of Scientific Ethics

Associated with "scientific ethics" is a kind of optimism,
which is not uncommon, for instance, among those followers of John Dewey's pragmatism who have a boundless
faith in the philosophy of social engineering. Science, it
is said, makes possible a control of the environment
through which man can, in principle, solve all his problems. The ardent believer in "scientific ethics" tends to
overlook the precarious factors in our social knowledge.
He has forgotten moreover that knowledge itself, as Ecclesiastes said, may finally bring sorrow.

Scientific knowledge can sometimes be as impotent to
change the course of social events as astronomical knowledge is to alter the moon's orbit of motion. Self-under-

standing may be powerless to alter the social environment. Let us suppose that a great analyst like Freud has succeeded in clarifying all the unconscious causative processes that are operative within him. Or let us suppose that Spinoza, a free man, succeeded in replacing all his inadequate ideas with adequate ones. Then let us imagine that some such self-comprehending man has been imprisoned within a concentration camp. He then sees human nature at its cruel and grovelling extremes. He realizes the impotence of his intelligence. Understanding all, he can yet do so little. If some masochist strain is strong within him, he may try to assure himself that he takes delight in the very intellectual understanding of the social process. Like Spinoza, he may seek some perverse comfort in the notion that Nature in her rich perfection manifests herself in all the possible varieties of cruelty. But of what real avail is "scientific ethics" in such a situation? What happiness can it bring to those who cannot escape a cruel, useless death?

An unreal optimism, an overestimation of itself, often accompanies "scientific ethics." It is a failure to realize how much of human decision is blind and how much human experience is beyond the capacities of scientific reconstruction. Recently a physician in New Hampshire was believed to have ended the life of a hopelessly suffering, cancer-ridden patient. The Communist newspaper in New York criticized this alleged act in strong terms; it declared its scientific optimism in an editorial: "There are no incurable diseases. Euthanasia is the very opposite of science because it talks in terms of incurable disease . . . What is needed more than anything else is a national program to eliminate the evils of our profit system which breeds disease, hunger, and poverty."[68] This was a metaphysics of scientific wish-fulfillment carried to its extreme. It virtually affirmed that the capitalist system was the cause of death itself; the social revolution, it argued, will abolish the facts of catabolism.

The contribution of scientific analysis to freedom is real; it liberates us from extraneous unconscious influences and makes us more fully aware of our own values. But when all this is done, there remains the world outside us, largely uncontrollable and unintelligible. Freud labored for self-understanding; he was at the end, none the less, an unhappy, pessimistic man. The world of war, conflict, and death is a surd datum which no philosophy can exorcise. We can understand why Freud in his last years grew sceptical as to the possibilities of therapy.

Scientific method in ethics does not provide us with what we can, together with common sense, call a philosophy of life. What is a philosophy of life? It is an assessment of what the chances are of man's realizing his values in this universe. It is necessarily speculative, since an attempt is made to answer questions whose solutions are indeterminate. Men will venture answers in blindness; the deep pessimist will hope, as he begets children, that his philosophy is wrong. Every momentous, actual choice is, however, related to some philosophy of life. The latter is composed of two ingredients. It incorporates an ethical theory, our self-conscious awareness of our values, and secondly, as we have mentioned, it judges the status of these values in the world in which we make our choices. After an ethical theory has been worked out, the actual problems of life are still unsolved, because the indeterminacies in our knowledge of the world are still with us. But some philosophy of life we must have. The human race is like the impatient boy who in reading a novel must always look ahead to the last chapter to see how things turn out. Philosophers have this trait, too. Except that the universe may not fit into the form of a novel, and may not have an ending.

12. The Empiricist Repression of Ethical Questions

At the end, we are confronted with an indeterminacy as to the meaning of life. Ethical science can enlighten us, and make our politics wiser. But our place in the scheme of things, the ultimate significance of our actions, remains unknowable.

Empiricist philosophers will, of course, affirm that what we have said has no meaning. A leading spokesman for this school writes, for instance, that "there is no sense in asking what is the ultimate purpose of our existence, or what is the real meaning of life." It is, he asserts, "misleading to say that life has no meaning, for that suggests that the statement that life has a meaning is factually significant, but false; whereas the truth is that, in the sense in which it is taken in this context, it is not factually significant."[69]

Empiricists try to repress "meaningless" questions into the philosophic unconscious, but the criterion of meaningfulness is often a frail censor. Psychoanalysis speaks of the "return of the repressed," and the meaningless question returns, in some form, to even the empiricist consciousness. Is the world designed by a superior being, Ayer asks, and he answers: "there is no good reason for believing that there is any such superior being." Perhaps there are no good reasons for such a belief, but if reasons are asked for, then the question must be meaningful, even if unanswerable. If a deity exists, continues Ayer, its purpose is not ours. Again it may be that an indifferent deity exists; perhaps defeat and frustration are life's final destiny, and a basic hostility to our values pervades the universe. In any case, however, the questions concerning deity remain meaningful, and they have been asked and left unanswered by the empiricist.

The empiricist holds that his outlook is free from any

component of emotional projection. There is no occasion, he says, for emotional attitudes toward meaningless questions; there is no basis for romantic cynicism or despair. But behind the empiricist epistemology, we find, upon analysis, a curious emotional decision; it transpires that the empiricist doctrine is founded not on logic but upon emotion. The empiricist declares that an unanswerable question is meaningless. What lies behind this definition or convention? It is a certain feeling of austerity, of self-laceration. The empiricist chooses, to his mind, "freely," a theory of meaning which adjudges unanswerable questions to be meaningless. He tells himself that the "meaningless-ness" of questions is no matter for regret since, after all, he didn't expect an answer anyhow. The underlying uncon-scious process is something like the following: "I will the meaninglessness of certain questions myself," says the empiricist, "since according to my own freely chosen theory of meaning, I may classify unanswerable questions as meaningless." A component of projection in empiricist thinking thus proceeds from a self-destructive impulse. The meaningless question is the element in the empiricist self which he would extirpate. And much in the style of empiricist writing reminds one of an effort to take delight in the technical virtuosity with which the job of self-destruction is done; it is as if one is being called upon to admire, at least, the unrelenting severity with which the author will destroy the meaning of his question.

The impulse of self-destruction, the death impulse, is strong in our time, and in the empiricist philosophy, it takes the masochist form of immolation on a theory of meaning. And the definition of the unanswerable as the meaningless bears resemblance to that neurotic pattern which Freud called "the omnipotence of thought"—the belief that our wishes, our psychic processes, are all-powerful in determining realities. The workings of "omnipotence of thought" in animistic and religious conceptions and idealistic metaphysics are well known. More covert, however, is the manner in which it operates in the empiricist theory of meaning. The death-wishes of the empiricist are turned inward against himself. The empiricist, if he dares to ask the meaning of life, turns upon himself to repress the question, like an adolescent boy trying to be tough. The theory of meaning provides the rationalization for the repression of the intrusive question. And the empiricist then avers himself as positively pleased by the outcome; the value-system of masochism is the decision-base for the postulates of his theory of knowledge.

The empiricist himself cannot avoid stating some sort of ethical outcome for his philosophy, though in strict logic, he should venture no such conclusion. But the necessity of choice in an indeterminate world obtrudes, choices which are made against the vast penumbra of unanswerable questions. Ayer thus writes: "In the last resort, therefore, each individual has the responsibility of choice; and it is a responsibility that is not to be escaped."[70] What sense, however, do these statements make from the empiricist standpoint? If the responsibility of choice is not to be escaped, it is because man makes choices just as he breathes, out of biological necessity. But if that is so, why speak of his "responsibility"? That makes as little sense as if we were to say: "each individual has the responsibility of breathing; and it is a responsibility that is not to be escaped." If "responsibility," on the other hand, connotes the judgment that the person *ought* to choose, then an unfounded ethical imperative has been deduced from empiricist doctrine, and in that case, furthermore, the responsibility could be escaped by the individual's failure to conform to the imperative. If the empiricist still wishes to maintain that choice-making cannot be escaped, he can do so now only by translating his hortatory statement into the necessary tautology that we choose what we choose; it is also true, however, that what we don't choose, we don't choose. These statements are inescapable, but also trivial, and are no ground for an ethical theory.

We make statements such as "each individual has the responsibility of choice" because we are aware that the outcome of decisions in historical crises are indeterminate. We cannot calculate what the individual contribution to history is; that, too, is indeterminate. But we do know too that there is no demonstrable theory which can dispose of the individual contribution as null. If it is possible for individuals to realize their values in history, they will be able to do so only if they are animated by a faith in themselves and a zest for action. And if it is possible for men to make their history, they can do so only through making the experiment. How far it is possible we cannot tell. We are responsible for our choice because we can appeal to no historical necessity for its decrees. Choice is the self-awareness of human response to the indeterminacies of historical events in the making.

References

1. Webb, Sidney: What happened in 1931: A record. *Political Quart.*, *II*:1, 16, 1932. Also, Lee, Jennie: *This Great Journey*. New York, Farrar & Rinehart, 1942, p. 117.
2. Mill, John Stuart: *Utilitarianism.* New York, Everyman's Edition, 1944, p. 4.
3. Russell, Bertrand: *Religion and Science.* New York, Holt, 1935, p. 243.
4. Locke, John: *An Essay Concerning Human Understanding*, Book I. London, George Rutledge and Sons, Chap. III, p. 39, paragraph 22.
5. Cf., Barber, Bernard: Acculturation and messianic movements. *Am. Soc. Rev.*, *VI*:663 ff., 1941.
6. Eggers, Dorothy: The signicance of dreams for anthropological research. *Am. Anthropol.*, *51*:177, 1949. Also, Eggers, Dorothy: The manifest content of dreams: A challenge to social science. *Am. Anthropol.*, *54*:478-479, 1952.

7. Dollard, John: *Caste and Class in a Southern Town.* New Haven, Yale, 1937, p. 384.

8. Zimmern, Helen, transl.: *The Philosophy of Nietzsche.* New York, Random, p. 384.

9. Brinton, Crane: *Nietzsche.* Cambridge, Harvard, 1941, p. 53.

10. Miller, H. Crichton: *Psychoanalysis and its Derivatives,* 2nd Ed. London, Oxford, 1945, p. 97.

11. The ethical use of the word "authentic" is found in the vocabulary of the "real revolutionary, the authentic scientist," Max Gottlieb, as depicted in Lewis, Sinclair: *Arrowsmith.* Cf., p. 136, 279. (Sartre has made the word central in the existentialist ethics.)

12. Dudley, Donald R.: *A History of Cynicism.* London, Methuen, 1937, p. x, xi.

13. *Essays of Arthur Schopenhauer,* transl. by T. Bailey Saunders. New York, A. L. Burt Company, p. 394.

14. Schopenhauer, Arthur: *The World as Will and Idea,* Vol. I, transl. by R. B. Haldane and J. Kemp. London, Kegan Paul, Trench, Trubner, 1896, p. 490-493.

15. Sully, James: *Pessimism,* 2nd Ed. London, Henry S. King & Co. 1891, p. 449, 451.

16. Wallace, W.: *Life of Arthur Schopenhauer.* London, Walter Scott, 1890, p. 190, 194.

17. Wallace, W.: *op. cit.,* p. 97.

18. Stevenson, Charles Leslie: *Ethics and Language.* New Haven, Yale Univ. Press, 1944, p. 36.

19. Veblen, Thorstein: *Absentee Ownership,* New York, B. W. Huebsch, 1923, p. 325.

20. Merton, Robert K.: *Mass Persuasion: The Social Psychology of a War Bond Drive.* New York, Harper, 1946, p. xi.

21. Fite, Warner: *Moral Philosophy.* New York, Dial Press, 1925, p. 201.

22. Stevenson, Charles Leslie: *Ethics and Language. Loc. cit.,* p. 82, 161.

23. Mill, John Stuart: *Utilitarianism. Loc. cit.,* p. 29.

24. Holmes, Oliver Wendell, Jr.: Collected Legal Papers, New York, Harcourt, Brace, 1921, p. 174.

25. Stevenson, Charles Leslie: *op. cit.,* p. 250, 110.

26. *Ibid.,* p. 164, 110.

27. The two conceptions of ethics correspond to two opposed patterns of personality. The traditional ethics of anxiety-inducers reflects the personality which is basically hierarchical, authoritarian, exploitative in parent-child relationships, and power-directed. The happiness ethics of free men, on the other hand, expresses the pattern of the affectionate, basically egalitarian personality. Cf., Adorno, T. W., Frenkel-Brunswik, Else, Levinson, Daniel J., and Sanford, R. Nevitt: *The Authoritarian Personality.* New York, Harper, 1950, p. 971.

28. Huxley, Julian: *Touchstone for Ethics.* New York, Harper, 1947, p. 213.
29. Frank, Lawrence K.: *Society as the Patient.* New Brunswick, Rutgers, 1948, p. 231.
30. Sjahrir, Soetan: *Out of Exile.* New York, Day, 1949, p. 67, 77.
31. Nehru, Jawaharlal: *Toward Freedom.* New York, Day, 1941, p. 315-317.
32. An illuminating discussion of the psychological basis of Gandhi's ethics of submission is contained in de Grazia, Sebastian: Mahatma Gandhi: The son of his mother. *Political Quart. XIX:*336ff., 1948.
33. Sjahrir, Soetan: *op. cit.,* p. 13.
34. The great similarity of the methods of Freud and Spinoza is the subject of an essay by Bernard, Walter: Freud and Spinoza. *Psychiatry, 9:*99, 1946.
35. de Spinoza, Benedict: *Ethics,* Book IV. Scholium, Prop. XVIII, Prop. XXIII. Also, Book V, Prop. III. In Wild, John, Ed.: *Spinoza Selections,* transl. by W. H. White. New York, Scribner, 1930.
36. Cf., de Spinoza, Benedict: *Ethics,* Book IV, Scholium, Prop. XLV, Prop. LIII, Prop. LXVII. *Ibid.*
37. A distinguished social psychologist has written that "the concept of attitudes is probably the most distinctive and indispensable concept in contemporary American psychology. No other term appears more frequently in experimental and theoretical literature." Allport, Gordon W.: The psychology of participation. *Psychol. Rev., 53:*117, 1945. Also, cf., Allport, Gordon W.: Attitudes, in *A Handbook of Social Psychology,* edited by Carl Murchison. Worchester, Clark Univ. Press, 1935, p. 798.
38. Moore, George Edward: *Principia Ethica.* Cambridge Univ. Press, 1929, p. 188, 203.
39. Veblen, Thorstein: *Theory of the Leisure Class.* New York, Viking, 1943, p. 152.
40. Freud, Sigmund: *Collected Papers,* Vol. II, 3rd Ed., transl. by Joan Riviere. London, Hogarth Press, 1942, p. 41, 92.
41. Russell, Bertrand: *Sceptical Essays.* New York, Norton, 1928, p. 111.
42. Stevenson, Charles Leslie: *op. cit.,* p. 1.
43. Mill, John Stuart: The works of Bentham. *Westminster Rev.,* July, 1838, p. 231, 252.
44. Plato: Protagoras, in *The Dialogues of Plato,* transl. by B. Jowett, 4th Ed., Vol. I. Oxford, Clarendon Press, 1953, p. 172.
45. Freud, Sigmund: Observations on "wild" psychoanalysis, in *Collected Papers,* Vol. II. *Loc. cit.,* p. 301-302.
46. de Spinoza, Benedict: *Ethics,* Book IV. Proposition XIV, *loc. cit.*
47. Odets, Clifford: *Waiting for Lefty,* in *Six Plays.* New York, Modern Library, 1939, p. 30-31.

48. Shaw, Bernard: *The Quintessence of Ibsenism.* New York, Brentano, 1904, p. 17-18.
49. Flügel, John Carl: *The Psychoanalytic Study of the Family,* 2nd Ed. London, Hogarth Press, 1926, p. 128.
50. Bradley, F. H.: *Ethical Studies.* Oxford, Clarendon Press, 1927, p. 196, 201.
51. Santayana, George: *Winds of Doctrine.* New York, Scribner, 1913, p. 189.
52. Freud, Sigmund: *New Introductory Lectures on Psychoanalysis,* transl. by W. J. H. Sprott. New York, Norton, 1933, p. 90, 95.
53. Mill, John Stuart: *Utilitarianism. Loc. cit.,* p. 6.
54. *Ibid.,* p. 29, 31.
55. Buckle, George Earle: *The Life of Benjamin Disraeli,* Vol. V. New York, Macmillan, 1920, p. 501.
56. Freud, Sigmund: *Collected Papers,* Vol. IV, 3rd Ed. transl. by Joan Riviere. London, Hogarth Press, 1946, p. 39-40.
57. Mill, John Stuart: *Autobiography.* London, Oxford, 1924, p. 113.
58. *Ibid.,* p. 123.
59. *Ibid.,* p. 125.
60. *Ibid.,* p. 92, 114, 43.
61. *Ibid.,* p. 121-122.
62. *Ibid.,* p. 120-121.
63. *Ibid.,* p. 120-121.
64. *Ibid.,* p. 41.
65. The perceptive historian, Halevy, comments: "This utilitarian is a Stoic, even an ascetic, and we cannot fail to recognize in his instinctive asceticism the stamp of his early education." Halevy, Elie: *A History of the English People in 1815,* Book III. London, Penguin, 1938, p. 90.
66. Halevy, Elie: *The Growth of Philosophic Radicalism,* transl. by Mary Morris. London, Macmillan, 1928, p. 84.
67. *Ibid.,* p. 510.
68. *The Daily Worker,* Jan. 9, 1950.
69. Ayer, A. J.: The claims of philosophy, in *Reflections on Our Age: Lectures Delivered at the Opening Session of Unesco.* New York, Columbia Univ. Press, 1949, p. 59.
70. *Ibid.,* p. 63.

PART TWO

CRITIQUE OF FREUD'S PHILOSOPHY OF CIVILIZATION

1. The Sense of Guilt: Its Social Conditions

WITHOUT knowledge as to ultimates, man can at least clarify and use his values to achieve his own human happiness. Ethics, as we have seen, becomes the applied social science which is employed with this aim. The achievement of a civilization is, from our standpoint, measured by its relative attainment of happiness. There is, however, a whole school of thought which regards the notion of happiness as delusive, and which alleges that civilization can realize only the unhappiness of men. An ancient tradition holds that wisdom is renunciation. In Freud's writings, tradition's verdict against civilizatiton has been stated in a magisterial idiom. A theory of liberal civilization will not be worth much if it cannot withstand Freud's criticisms. To these therefore, we now turn our attention.

The sense of guilt, according to Freud, is the Nemesis of civilization. "The price of progress in civilization is paid in forfeiting happiness through the heightening of the sense of guilt."[1] Civilization, says Freud, is based on the renunciation of instinctual satisfaction; cultural privation, he states, "dominates the whole field of social relations between human beings."[2] The prohibition against incest is part of civilized life, and Freud holds that this prohibition was "perhaps the most maiming wound ever inflicted throughout the ages on the erotic life of man."[3] Add to this the barriers of monogamy, and "the sexual life of man," Freud concludes, "is seriously disabled, whatever

72

we may say."[4] Superimposed on this disability is the sense of guilt. Its roots are in the so-called Oedipus complex, the sexual longing of the son for his mother, but its dramatic entry in human history took place when the primal father was murdered by an association of brothers. This is the myth of the origin of remorse. The primal father was both hated and loved; there was an ambivalence of feeling toward him. Remorse was born because a loved person was killed. Moreover, each generation experiences anew the same impulses of aggression toward its fathers. Feelings of guilt persist, and are reinforced with the repressive efforts of each generation's conscience. "Guilt," says Freud, "is the expression of the conflict of ambivalence, the eternal struggle between Eros and the destructive or death instinct."[5]

The growth of civilization, Freud argues, must intensify the sense of guilt. The advancement of civilization extends the emotional range of human society; it begins with the family, it ends by embracing the whole of humanity. The conflict of ambivalence, Freud believes, becomes more acute with the increasing size of human groups, "until perhaps the sense of guilt may swell to a magnitude that individuals can hardly support." The growth of civilization is contrary to man's instinctive needs because it involves the magnified frustration of man's aggressive nature. The aggression of men toward each other, Freud affirms, is an "innate, independent, instinctual disposition." The aim of civilization is to bind all men together by some great tie of affection, to constitute a common humanity, and Freud holds: "the natural instinct of aggressiveness in man, the hostility of each one against all and of all against each one, opposes this programme of civilization . . ."[6]

Humankind, according to Freud, is caught in a destructive dilemma. On the one hand, it can choose to suppress its tendency toward aggression. But this will result in a heightening of the sense of guilt, for guilt is aggressive energy which has been turned inward against one's self. Or, on the other hand, we can give vent to our aggressive desires. In that case, the enterprise of civilization is defeated. Men have only two alternatives: either the weary, energy-consuming, ever growing burden of internal guilt, or the suspense, dangers, and fears of external aggression. To Freud's mind, no real solution of this dilemma is possible. A communist society, he believes, can only endure so long as it has an outlet for aggressive impulses. But when this outlet is gone, what then? What will communist societies do when there are no longer kulaks to denounce, when there is no longer a capitalist encirclement against which an eternal vigilance is to be maintained? The bourgeois scapegoat, in Freud's view, is the psychological safety-valve for the communist society. "One only wonders, with some concern, however, how the Soviets will manage when they have exterminated their bourgeois entirely."[7] Universal love could be propounded as an ideal to the Christian community only so long as there was a convenient body of non-Christians against whom hatred could be expended in socially approved ways. A universal civilization, however, according to Freud, would place an intolerable burden of guilt, of repression, upon its members. World peace would bring psychological catastrophe. What can a theory of liberal civilization reply to Freud?

In the first place, let us ask whether a sense of guilt is indeed a pervasive trait of all cultures. Is the conviction of guilt a basic attribute of all human civilizations? Literary evidence indicates that there are significant variations in society's sense of guilt; at times, it is hardly more than a vestigial phenomenon. Contrast England in the Restoration and the eighteenth century with England in the mid-seventeenth century; on the one hand, a gay hedonistic, happiness-loving people, and on the other, a people which

knew the torments of remorse.[8] The England of Tom
Jones, of Daniel Defoe's characters, is one in which dark
shadows are dissipated: the affections, joys, and sense of
adventure have begun to well up. The Calvinist interlude
recedes, with its anguish of damnation and predestination.
Sects of Unitarians and Quakers have begun to attract
adherents, and their theology, we might say, has alleviated
the harshness of the deified super-ego. God has become
friendlier with men, and is less the sadistic predestinator.
The religion of cruelty gives way to tolerant, gentle creeds.
The leaders in religious thought are pioneers who detach
their creeds from underpinnings in guilt-experience. A
sense of happiness replaces the heavy atmosphere of gloom.
At the close of the Middle Ages, the historian Huizinga
tells us, a sombre melancholy weighed on people's minds.
There was a widespread sadness, and it was bad form to
dare to praise what life had to offer. The "sum" of human
happiness can change from one period to another, and the
liberation of energies which began with the Renaissance
increased the human awareness and capacity for joy.[9]

The great eras of civilization are those in which the
sense of happiness is strong, in which the courage of reason
is high, and in which men feel no guilt for their human
status. Such were the times of Elizabethan England and
the Athens of Pericles; their philosophers were men like
Bacon and Anaxagoras who believed that reason could
make happiness accessible to men on earth. Under what
social conditions might we expect the sense of guilt to
diminish?

2. Fathers and Sons: The Guilt of the Generations

The persistence of guilt-feelings, according to Freud's
analysis, is due to the recurrent conflict of generations. The
clash between fathers and sons repeats itself with each
period; to the older generation, the younger has some-

thing of Turgenev's nihilist, whereas the latter regards its elders as subsisting on antiquated notions by virtue of their authority. But this conflict is not of a sustained equal intensity. It is strongest in the patriarchal society, with its static, immobile ways. The tremendous tensions of patriarchal dominance called forth the commandment to honor thy father and thy mother.[10] The nomadic pastoral economy concentrated the ownership of the flocks in the father's hands; the young men, angry and restless, labored for years as Jacob did to win some share. Resentment seethed among the suppressed sons. A society which was a gerontocracy evoked responses of frustrated aggression, like the attempt of Jacob's sons to wreak vengeance upon Joseph, their father's favorite.

A society which allows its youth in the fullness of their powers to find an opportunity for their energies will harbor a minimum of repressed aggressive impulses toward the older generation. Under such conditions, hatred toward the father is at a minimum; there is an absence of ambivalence. The values of men, their religion, cease to be dominated by images of cruelty. The young men who made the American Revolution were, as Thomas Jefferson, largely hedonistic-minded; they rejected the Calvinist god, and speculated of a benign deity. The Declaration of Independence was a landmark in the history of political philosophy because it was the first State document which made the "pursuit of happiness" an inalienable right of man, which it was the purpose of governments to safeguard. The discovery of happiness as the ultimate end of political society was the work of a revolutionary generation which had liberated itself from the sanctions of the sense of guilt.[11] Energies wasted in suppressing the rebellion of human drives revealed themselves in full creative amplitude. A distinguished historian of ideas writes: "This was more than a new principle of government, it was a new principle of life which was thus proposed and officially indorsed. The most that could be asked from governments of the Old World was to promote virtue and to maintain justice; honor, 'amor patriae' and fear were the essential principles on which rested the governments described by Montesquieu. But in spite of the eternal and unquenchable thirst for happiness in the heart of every man, what European, what Frenchman particularly, could openly and officially maintain that the 'pursuit of happiness' was a right, and that happiness could be reached and truly enjoyed? This quest of happiness had been the main preoccupation of French philosophers during the eighteenth century, but in spite of their philosophical optimism, they were too thoroughly imbued with pessimism ever to think that it was possible to be happy; . . . The whole Christian civilization had been built on the idea that happiness is neither desirable nor obtainable in this vale of tears and affliction. The Declaration of Independence, on the contrary, placed human life on a new axis by maintaining that happiness is a natural right of the individual and the whole end of government."[12]

A society in which emotions and talents are not repressed does not hesitate to avow happiness as its end. It is not impelled to install inauthentic values as its guides—the reflection of its own warped life. A free society, in this sense, is not affected at its core by the primal ambivalence which is the source of the guilt-experience. The younger generation doesn't find hatred interwoven with love as a basic feeling toward the old; its constructive impulses are not deflected into an urge to destroy. The sense of guilt had receded to minor proportions in a thinker like Jefferson who could say simply, "I too am an Epicurean," and have done with Calvin's proposal to deify a "daemon of malignant spirit" in place of the "benevolent Governor of the world."[13]

3. **The Guilt of Social Status**

The conflict of generations is, however, only one source of guilt-experience in society. Guilt-experience, as Freud said, arises from a conflict of ambivalent feelings, from the strife of love and hatred for the same persons. Such situations of ambivalent feeling are not confined to the relations between fathers and sons. They are found in the relations between economic classes, religious groups, between men and women. Guilt-experience makes its appearance in all those social relations where incompatible attitudes of affection and hostility dwell in an unstable co-existence. The existence of class exploitative systems has thus been a major social cause of the sense of guilt, one which has weighed grimly upon the sensitive young of the upper classes. For class systems make for ambivalences; whereas youthful affections are open and spontaneous, the imperative of the class system, however disguised, is to hate your inferiors. Movements of social revolution have therefore provided the means whereby youth have sought to alleviate their consciousness of guilt. The annals of English and Russian revolutionary history are abundant illustration of this struggle with guilt-experience.

In her great autobiography, *My Apprenticeship,* Beatrice Webb asked why persons like herself, reared to wealth and comfort, had undertaken to promote a socialist agitation. The English workers, after the defeat of the Chartist movement, had sunk into a brutalized apathy. The initiative for social reform came from members of the upper class. What accounts for this strange social fact? Beatrice Webb's answer takes one to the heart of the problem of guilt:

"The origin of the ferment is to be discovered in a new consciousness of sin among men of intellect and men of property; a consciousness at first philanthropic and practical—Oastler, Shaftesbury, and Chadwick; then literary and artistic—Dickens, Carlyle, Ruskin and finally, analytic, historical and explanatory—in his latter days John Stuart Mill; Karl Marx and his English interpreters; Alfred Russel Wallace and Henry George; Arnold Toynbee and the Fabians. I might perhaps add a theological category—Charles Kingsley, F. D. Maurice, General Booth and Cardinal Manning. 'The sense of sin has been the starting-point of progress' was during these years, the oft-repeated saying of Samuel Barnett, rector of St. Jude's, Whitechapel, and founder of Toynbee Hall.

"When I say consciousness of sin, I do not mean the consciousness of personal sin: . . . The consciousness of sin was a collective or class consciousness; a growing uneasiness, amounting to conviction, that the industrial organisation, which had yielded rent, interest, and profits on a stupendous scale, had failed to provide a decent livelihood and tolerable conditions for a majority of the inhabitants of Great Britain. . . . This class-consciousness of sin was usually accompanied by devoted personal service, sometimes by open confession and a deliberate dedication of means and strength to the reorganisation of society on a more equalitarian basis. One of the noblest and most original of these latter-day confessors, Arnold Toynbee, expressed, on the eve of his premature death—in words charged, it may be overcharged, with emotion—at once his penitence and his hope for a nobler life for the mass of his fellow-countrymen. 'We—the middle classes, I mean, not merely the very rich—we have neglected you; instead of justice, we have offered you charity, and instead of sympathy we have offered you hard and unreal advice; but I think we are changing. If you would only believe it and trust us, I think that many of us would spend our lives in your service. You have—I say it clearly and advisedly— you have to forgive us, for we have wronged you; we have sinned against you grievously—not knowingly always, but still we have sinned' . . ."[14]

Almost at the same time as the events which Beatrice Webb describes in England, a tremendous wave of consciousness of social guilt was awakening the Russian youth with its ferment. The autobiography of the great anarchist, Prince Kropotkin, re-creates the atmosphere of the years of social dedication:

"Five years later, thousands and thousands of the Russian youth—the best part of it—were doing the same. Their watchword was 'V naród' (To the people; be the people). During the years 1860-1865, in nearly every wealthy family a bitter struggle was going on between the fathers, who wanted to maintain the old traditions, and the sons and daughters, who defended their right to dispose of their lives according to their own ideals. Young men left the military service, the counter, the shop, and flocked to the university towns. Girls, bred in the most aristocratic families, rushed penniless to St. Petersburg, Moscow, and Kieff, eager to learn a profession. . . . After hard and bitter struggles, many of them won that personal freedom. Now they wanted to utilize it, not for their own personal enjoyment, but for carrying to the people the knowledge that had emancipated them. In every town of Russia, . . . small groups were formed for self-improvement and self-education. . . . The aim of all that reading and discussion was to solve the great question which rose before them. In what way could they be useful to the masses? Gradually, they came to the idea that the only way was to settle amongst the people, and to live the people's life."[15]

Liberal social movements have been fed by the desire to assuage the sense of guilt which is the outcome of social inequalities. This mode of guilt-experience arises, as we

have said, from the conflict of ambivalent feelings, between emotions of love and hatred for the same objects.
It is to be distinguished from the other type of guilt-
experience, that which is the consequence of a tension
between the self and conscience, between ego and super-
ego. The guilt of ambivalence is thus differentiated from
the guilt of conscience. The latter arises from the unconscious fear of authority; it is the expression of internalized authoritarian standards. Conscience, as Freud states,
exercises the functions of a censor; it watches and judges
the person's actions. "The sense of guilt, the severity of
the super-ego, is therefore the same thing as the rigour of
conscience."[16] The guilt, however, which we feel when we
hurt somebody we love does not involve a reference to
the conscience or super-ego. It is our affection expressing
itself in anger against that part of ourselves which has hurt
the loved person; parental affection leads one to resist an
attack on one's child, and parental affection likewise re-
proaches us for harsh behavior toward the child. The
guilt-experience of ambivalent feelings is founded on an
empathically felt pain in a person both loved and hated.
The lover hates himself for the pain he has brought to his
beloved. And this is the most basic mode of guilt-experience, the one which social movements seek somehow to
reduce.

Liberal social movements have thus been based on the
effort to broaden the areas of social feeling. They have
been directed against those aspects of the social system
which make for ambivalences rather than simple social
affections. Under the system of serfdom, for instance, landlords could never permit themselves the thought "that
their serfs were endowed with just as 'elevated and refined'
feelings as their own." It was the achievement of such a
writer as Turgenev that his works "succeeded in planting

in the landlords' hearts the thoughts that the serfs were capable of feeling exactly like the owners. Before their time such an admission would have been regarded as a debasement of the lofty 'gentlemen's' feelings."[17] Thus likewise the novels of Dickens made the lives of ordinary people, their tragedies and comedies, part of the proper subject of literature. In our own time, Alan Paton in *Cry The Beloved Country* has brought forth the depth of meaning in the lives of the submerged Negro population of South Africa. By making it possible for the positive expression of affections to grow, by removing those social structures in which fester hatred and repression, liberal social movements reduce the collective consciousness of guilt which otherwise lies heavy on men. This is the therapy of social action.

4. The Guilt of Fratricide

The burden of inequality has then been the cardinal factor in man's consciousness of guilt. To this fact, the record of the Bible bears a strange and eloquent testimony. It is remarkable that guilt-experiences in the Bible do not center around some primal parricide. Instead, the recurrent theme is the hatred, jealousy, and deception of brothers, their envy and competition for their father's favor; the origin of the wars of peoples is the strife of brothers. The significance of these narratives as documents of philosophy of history is outstanding.

Cain and Abel, the farmer and the shepherd, contended for God's good will. The conflict between the pastoral nomads and the sedentary agriculturists is the key to much of the history of the ancient Middle East, and this legend expresses it in a simple dramatic diagram. The story, which is weighted in favor of the pastoralist, tries to justify the antagonism which the invading Hebrew nomads felt for the settled Canaanites. The guilt of the invaders is projected upon their victims, so that when Cain murders Abel, his punishment is not death but the everlasting mark of guilt. Jealousy, the child of social injustice, makes its historic appearance in mythologic form, and God warns Cain:

> "If your heart is honest, you would surely look bright? If you are sullen, sin is lying in wait for you, eager to be at you—yet you ought to master it."[18]

The story of Canaan's origin is likewise an attempt to appease guilt experiences. An intense guilt must have weighed upon the Hebrews as they exterminated the Canaanite tribes, and the series of Biblical myths was designed to convey the approval of the Hebraic super-ego. Thus the Canaanites were said to be descended from Ham, one of Noah's three sons, who alone had dared to look upon his nakedness. Noah had cursed his youngest son: "A curse upon Canaan! May he be slave and thrall to his brothers!" Thereby, the Hebrews' sense of guilt was to be alleviated with God's countersign upon their actions.

The inferior status of Ishmael, the ancestor of the Bedouin Arab tribes, was similarly attributed to the divine mandate. Ishmael and Isaac were both sons of Abraham, but the first was born of a handmaid. The father would have dealt kindly with Ishmael; he would have restrained the jealousy of Isaac's mother against the first born. To God, Abraham said: "Oh that Ishmael might be under thy care," but it was God himself who had ordained the birth of the chosen Isaac. God had chosen to make of Ishmael a lesser son, "a wild-ass of a man, his hand against everyone, and everyone's hand against him, defying all his kinsmen." The guilt of the Hebrew tribes is once more projected upon the divine will. They are freed from the responsibility of the inequality of peoples.

The tale of Esau and Jacob continues the efforts to solve the problem of the guilt-experience of inequality. Esau was according to this legend the ancestor of the Edomites, against whom the Hebrews were waging a savage war. The Hebrews were trying to drive the Edomites from the latter's ancestral land. By what right then should the sons of Esau be evicted and destroyed? Esau, answers the legend, was willing to sell his birthright for a mess of pottage, "so little store did Esau set by his birthright." But that scarcely lightens the Hebrews' burden of guilt. Rebekah, mother of the two brothers, is therefore made the responsible agent who was prepared to take upon herself any blame which would be directed against the younger son, Jacob. So Jacob was blessed by his father to inherit a land of corn and wine in plenty, with other nations as his servants, whereas Esau was fated to live by the sword, far from rich soil, and to serve his brother. The guilt of Jacob's deception was alleviated by recourse to the will of the parents. The device, however, was hardly convincing, and could scarcely have repressed the Hebrews' sense of guilt.

The oft-told story of Joseph and his brethren is another projective myth of the origin of human inequality. Joseph, says this legend, was the most beloved of Jacob's sons, the son of his old age and his favorite wife. He aroused the jealousy of the other brothers; he regarded himself as their superior. The brothers barely refrained from murdering him; they sold him into slavery. The final blessing, however, goes to Joseph, "the prince among his brothers," and Joseph's son, Ephraim. Joseph's brethren are assigned lesser destinies; Reuben, says the dying Jacob, will not fare well because he committed incest with his father's wife, Zebulun is to live by the sea, Gad will be a raider, and so on. Joseph is blessed with divine favor, for he saved the whole clan with Egyptian grain when famine was upon the land.

The tribal super-ego is thus invoked to justify the inequality among the Hebrew tribes themselves. An ideological narrative is invented to rationalize the unequal endowment among the brothers; some, it is held, were more deserving than others. Guilt was projected upon the underserving inferiors. When the brothers were asked for a hostage in Egypt, they saw their misfortune as a punishment for their crime against Joseph: "This misfortune has befallen us because we were guilty about our brother; we saw his misfortune, and we would not listen to his entreaties." It is amazing that throughout all the Biblical myths a proclivity to primal parricide does not assert itself; in this respect, the Biblical evidence does not confirm Freud's theory of the origins of culture and guilt. What we do find is that each generation reiterates the strife of brothers. The consciousness of guilt arises from the crimes of one brother against another; in every case, there is a competitive struggle among the brothers for the father's, or God's, preferential blessing. Impulses of human friendliness, of brotherly affection, from time to time, do escape the bonds of competitive conflict; Esau embraced Jacob, and they wept together when they met as mature men; the feared war did not take place. The ambivalent feelings of brothers toward each other, and their consequential sense of guilt, is the outcome of a patriarchal social system, which sets brothers against each other. Fratricide, not parricide, is the historic primal crime, the primary generative component of the social sense of sin.[19] And the tribal projective myths attempt their explications: to whom by historic decree will the patriarchal birthright go? Which sons by historic decree shall be slaves to a brother?

The fratricidal anxieties are deep seated in our world

civilization, the leading source of the contemporary consciousness of guilt. If a universal society is constructed
which diminishes fratricidal anxieties, men will suffer less
from guilt-experience. A universal civilization which erad-
icates exploitative classes and national rivalries, which
nurtures the sense of brotherhood in men, and provides
the setting of equality and individual freedom, will lift
the burden of guilt. There is no law of universal guilt
which embraces societies with its decree of affliction.
Freud's pessimism took the form of a projective philosophy
which made the sense of guilt essential to man as a creature
of culture. But social wisdom shows that a reconstruction
of society can liberate men in large measure, from guilt-
anxiety, and to that extent, make them the more blessed in
happiness.

5. The Compatibility of Sexuality and Culture

Does civilization involve, as Freud believed, the renunciation of instinctual gratification? The evidence on this
point belies Freud's answer. The measure of civilization
is the degree of joys and satisfactions it brings to men; and
advances in civilization have been advances in the happiness of people.

Freud's critique of civilization was based essentially on
the argument that the advent of culture entailed the
frustration of sexual and aggressive impulses. This very
emphasis is an indirect tribute to the achievement of
civilization. For there are other drives in human nature,
hunger, thirst, the need for shelter against the physical environment, the need for security. The exclusive concern
with sexual frustration indicates that other basic drives
have been satisfied with the development of civilization.
The locus of dissatisfaction, indeed, is now found in less
elemental needs. It is the struggle for food which dominates primitive life. Those who idealize the comforts of

primitive existence soon change their mind when they have shared the experience of unending anxiety over the day's food supply. Enthusiastic primitivists always get a jolt when they see such films as *Nanook of the North* or *Grass*. Hunger is more primordial in its psychological bearings than the sexual impulse. The evidence of legend and custom led Sir James G. Frazer to conclude: . . . "where the instinct of self-preservation, which manifests itself chiefly in the search for food, conflicts or appears to conflict with the instinct which conduces to the propagation of the species, the former instinct, as the primary and more fundamental, is capable of overmastering the latter. In short, the savage is willing to restrain his sexual propensity for the sake of food."[20] When food is the life-problem, men's fantasies of an after-life without anxiety have the character of Happy Hunting Grounds. A land flowing with milk and honey was the vision which moved the Hebrew freedmen through their wanderings in the desert. Men bereft of food will scheme and plot with a kind of madness; soldiers in isolated posts dreamed and talked of hamburgers and onions. The hungry and exhausted have little energy or interest in sexual activity; the famished, tired coolies in the South Pacific showed small concern for the proclivities of their women. Only a people well advanced in civilization is moved to enquire into the problem of a higher sexual contentment.

The advancement of civilization, moreover, has brought a recognition of the sexual contribution to happiness. That sexual joy is a primary source of happiness is acknowledged only at a late stage in the history of philosophic thought. Even the great thinkers of the seventeenth century, Leibniz, Spinoza, Descartes, were celibates; when love is central to their thinking as in Spinoza's case, it is love of the most sublimated kind for the universe as a whole. Of this love, Spinoza spoke with rare rapture,

"what a union! what a love!"; it is a love which unites us
so intimately with God "that it will not let us love anything beside him."[21] But human love, as such, is not something which stands high in Spinoza's values. For him as
for Freud, the conjunction of the organs of love with
those of excretion was a cause for sorrow.[22]

The tradition of philosophy ranked intellectual activity
highest in the scale of values. Such activity was pure,
unrelated to bodily need. The pleasures of the senses were
regarded as low-grade disturbers of the intellectual peace.
The philosophic tradition reflected all the influence of
institutions which had taught men that sexual desire was
evil, and which had impressed upon them the guilt of
Adam's fall and the Original Sin which was within themselves. Man's sexual life was disabled; the linkage of sexuality with evil was part of the projective intent of the
myth of the Virgin Birth, and it went so far as to require
an Immaculate Conception. But the advancement of civilization which began with the Industrial Revolution, the
concomitant weakening of repressive forces, has enabled
men to achieve a partial liberation of their capacities for
sexual happiness.

It was only in the eighteenth and nineteenth centuries
that philosophers realized a saner and healthier attitude
toward sexual joy. Diderot, for instance, in his *Voyage de
Bougainville* dwelled with approval on the solicitude
which the primitive maidens displayed for the sexual well-
being of their distinguished visitor. Philosophers began to
speak of women with love, and even ventured to get married. John Stuart Mill waited for twenty years in a Vic-
torian romance to marry Mrs. Harriet Taylor, and later
spoke of her as the inspirer of all that was best in his
thoughts. The unrestrained ardor with which he described
her influence embarrassed his friends. To Mill, however,
she was the full symbol of his personal happiness; if he had

known someone like her in his early years, he said, he would have been spared the severe mental crisis of his youth. She taught him the primacy of the emotions for man's happiness. Auguste Comte, his positivist contemporary, was undergoing a similar emotional discovery of woman. Clotilde de Vaux evoked in him a language of eulogistic metaphor which verged on metaphysics. With complete sincerity, the positivist philosopher wrote to his beloved: " My growth in universal love has encreased under the constant stimulus of our pure affection."[23]

Love and culture, Freud has maintained, are inevitably opposed in their interests. He writes: ". . . the conflict between civilization and sexuality is caused by the circumstance that sexual love is a relationship between two people, in which a third can only be superfluous or disturbing, whereas civilization is founded on relations between larger groups of persons. When a love-relationship is at its height no room is left for any interest in the surrounding world."[24] Culture is in opposition to love, says Freud, because it has to withdraw energy which might be monopolized by self-sufficient lovers, and distribute it through many social channels as "aim-inhibited libido." The experience of the thinkers we have mentioned directly confutes Freud's thesis. Diderot's love for Sophie Voland sustained him in his labors on the *Encyclopédie,* and Mrs. Taylor led Mill to include a chapter on the future of the laboring classes in his *Principles of Political Economy.* Sexual love made the social objectives and affections of these men more profound and extensive. This psychological truth is of considerable importance because it undermines an essential part of Freud's critique of civilization. The social feelings are themselves stimulated and nourished by satisfactory love experiences.

The fallacy in this portion of Freud's theory was his adoption of a kind of energy-fund, or libido-fund, doctrine. This fund, in Freud's conception, was fixed, so that if a large quantity was expended between two lovers, that quantity was to be subtracted from the fund; lovers would thus reduce the supply of available energy for the rest of society. The experience of lovers, according to Freud, would thus reduce the net friendliness available for ordinary social relations. But the truth of the matter is quite otherwise. A person who is frustrated in his deepest longings tends to become dejected and dispirited, uninterested in life and its activities. This is, indeed, the psychology of defeatism; the physiological basis of activity itself seems to have been lessened. Give to a person great personal happiness, however, and a resurgence of energy occurs. The lover and the social reformer are thus often conjoined. Shelley, who called upon his generation to fulfill a mission of social revolution, "Ye might arise and will," also called upon the Wild Spirit, the diffused cosmic energy of love.

Frustration withers the source of energy; joy and satisfaction nurture its growth. Sexual love, far from isolating people and separating society into islands, provides new, untapped energies for social relations of good-will. The lover, in his happiness, is proverbially known for the accession of friendliness and helpfulness in his character, just as the defeated lover is known for his embitteredness and withdrawal. The new depths of energy which love uncovers overflow into social relations generally. And it is this fact of human experience which was omitted from Freud's account of human nature.

With the advent of the Industrial Revolution, and the social changes which followed, philosophers no longer consigned sexual love to the nether region of sub-values. They began to recognize love as potentially the most intense of human experiences, and to perceive that other values were genuine in so far as they absorbed something of its emotion. Bernard Shaw expressed the underlying

feeling of this philosophic liberation with simple frank-
ness in a famous passage of autobiography: "I liked sexual
intercourse because of its amazing power of producing a
celestial flood of emotion and exaltation of existence
which, however momentary, gave me a sample of what may
one day be the normal state of being for mankind in intellectual ecstasy."[25] The discovery of the instinctive
sources of life had been made in its fullness. The task
of thought was now to help realize the liberation from the
taboos and distortions which historic agencies had imposed upon men. Civilization was now conceived as a
liberational force, not a repressive one; and institutions
which had built upon the thwarting of men's impulses
were recognized as having set men in hatred one against
another.

6. Social Sources of Sexual Disablement

A disablement of man's sexual life has, however, ensued
during the course of his history. What made it so easy for
the Christian-Platonic tradition to identify sexuality and
bodily joy with evil? Whence this sundering of man so
that he became ashamed of himself?

History attests the fact that man's shame is born of his
misery. The underfed, the oppressed, the humiliated,
come to hate life, to hate each moment of living to which
they are condemned; they curse each day which they must
live anew. Sexual joy demands a surplus of energy, the
fullness of affection, the overflowing of pleasure. But to
the tired and embittered, sexual activity becomes not an
occasion for love of another, but for the cruel venting of
aggression, contempt, or anger upon some woman, the indulgence of hatred for the submissive object. Sexual activity becomes dissociated from the experience of love,
becomes the means for the expression of hatred for humanity. And thus sexual activity becomes interfused with the

experience of guilt; for this most intimate ambivalent conjunction, this union of the most direct expressive love and hatred, gives rise to the most intense of guilt-feelings.

From the social conditions in the Greco-Roman world grew an ugly self-hatred of bodily life and physical energies. As Rostovtzeff describes it: "Hard life, hard work, meager prospects for the future, oppression from above—such was the lot of millions of peasants and of hundreds of thousands of workmen. No wonder that they sought refuge with the gods, and hoped, firmly hoped to fare better after the end of their dull human career on the earth, in the after life, in the mysterious other world."[26] The priests of the mystic cults fed the religiosity of the craving souls of the miserable. The Greco-Roman world was host to a variety of mystic vapors, Orphism, neo-Pythagoreanism, gnosticism, astrology, and Oriental doctrines of various kinds. Life on earth was regarded as unimportant, religion became preoccupied with salvation. The Pythagorean Savior, Apollo, promised succor to those who would succeed in escaping from the bodily portion of their humanity, the passions and material needs.

And from the philosophical ideas of the Greco-Romans, Paul imported into Christianity the identity of "flesh" with "sin."[27] "For I know that in me, that is, in my flesh, dwelleth no good thing." Mysticism, the notion of "to be in God" was not an authentic Jewish idea; Paul derived the emphasis on mystic union, of "life in Christ," from the mystery cults. "The spirit of God," said Paul, "dwelleth in you"; this species of mysticism regarded the body as alien to the divine, as something to be mortified. "For if ye live after the flesh, ye shall die; but if ye through the Spirit do mortify the deeds of the body, ye shall live."[28] Paul's accretions to Judaism made it possible for Christianity to become the Roman world-religion.

Asceticism, the self-hatred of the body, arises in communities where sadistic sensual indulgence has likewise reached a high point. It has been observed that the greatest exponents of the chaste life have often been profligates before their conversion. Guilt-experience went deep into Roman life. The command "Love thine enemies" was addressed to a society where cruelty was well embedded in the institutional fabric. Sexual activity was associated with cruelty to slaves, to one's inferiors—the debasement of women by acts connected with excretory organs. With ascetic revulsion, Augustine had characterized the process of birth: "inter foeces et urinam nascimur." Men who experienced cruelty and debasement toward themselves in their daily lives would regard sexual experience as a way of reacting with cruelty and debasement toward others. Love was transmuted into physical loathing and aggression. The sadism of Greco-Roman society, expressed in its mode of sexual behavior, brought its by-product of guilt-experience.

Sexual life can be disabled even where sexual indulgences are promiscuous, and even where the cultural super-ego, the conscience, is absent or weak. For where sexual activity is the means whereby the individual temporarily obliterates his despair, it becomes the emotional vehicle of cruelty and hatred. The experience of the Negro people in our own society is a tragic instance of this general truth. The depressed segment of the Negro community may lead "freer" sexual lives than white people, yet its incidence of mental illness is considerably higher. The stereotype of the "happy Negro" arises. As an acute social scientist writes: "the white caste have the satisfactions that go with mastery, superiority, control, maturity, and duty well-fulfilled. . . . The Negroes, on the other hand, get much more and much freer direct impulse satisfaction."[29] But as Abram Kardiner has said: "The Negro is hardly the abandoned sexual hedonist he is supposed to be." Loss of self-respect in the social world is the basis for the high proportion of sexual disorders among the Negro lower classes.

Promiscuous sexual gratification may be greater among the impoverished Negro group than among white people, but it is also attended by a greater unhappiness. Multiple sexual objects do not coincide with the meaning of sexual freedom. For what characterizes the sexual activity of the submerged class is what has been called "the mark of oppression"—the influence on their sexual experience of the inequality, fear, suffering, and indignities which they sustain in their social life.[30] Sexual activity tends to become violent, aggressive, fitful, something which is dissociated from feelings of tenderness. Sexual activity is then not the occasion of joyful experience, but a brief opportunity to dominate another person or a moment of sensory escape from a world which one would repress. If Freud were correct in linking sexual desire to aggressive instinct, then the degree of frustration among the Negroes should be small, and their incidence of mental illness low. But it is precisely the use of sexual relations as the implement of aggressive tendencies which is an index of the frustration which the caste system inflicts upon the Negro; sexual life is maimed, and ascetic rejections of sexuality are then the expression of the guilt of hatred. Sexual disablement is an aspect of a social system which has not yet outgrown the patterns of oppression. Sexual disablement is the mark of a society which has not succeeded in civilization.

7. Reply to Sexual Pessimism

Freud's pessimism as to the possibilities of happiness was only in part founded on his reflections concerning the frustrational character of civilization. In the last analysis, Freud believed, "something in the nature of the sexual instinct itself is unfavorable to the achievement of absolute gratification."[31] Like Schopenhauer, Freud held that the sexual instinct always deceives human beings; it promises happiness, it brings delusion. Did Freud, however, project as universal traits of the sexual drive factors which are limited to the workings of specific social institutions? Civilization can hope to alter social forms which frustrate people, but if it is faced with traits inherent in the sexual drive, it must probably resign itself to the biological unhappiness of men. The question then is whether Freud underestimated the possibilities in the therapy of a social, liberal reconstruction. What then are the grounds which Freud adduces to explain the sexual unhappiness of men? Are they inherent in the nature of the sexual impulse? Or can they be modified so as to liberate human capacities for happiness?

Psychical impotence, says Freud, is widespread. It arises from a dualism, a separation, which culture inflicts on men's emotional lives. A happy sexual outlook would combine affectionate with sensual feelings for the same person. But culture, says Freud, divides the erotic life of men into two components, "the same two that are personified in art as heavenly and earthly (or animal love)." What men love, they do not desire, and what they desire, they do not love. The psychical impotence which arises consists in an inability to summon into sexual activity the whole mental energy which belongs to that instinct. "It is capricious, easily upset, often clumsily carried out, and not very pleasurable. Above all, however, it avoids all associations with feelings of tenderness."[32] All this, Freud holds, stems from the influence of the restrictions on incest, the restrictions on the child's or adolescent's first sexual objects. The compulsion of this taboo then prompts men to direct their sensual feelings only to those who don't remind them of their mother. Women who are not the objects of tenderness can be suitable objects for degradation in sexual desire. "Full sexual satisfaction only comes when he can give himself up wholeheartedly to enjoyment, which with his well-brought-up wife, for instance, he does not venture to do. Hence comes his need for a less exalted sexual object, a woman ethically inferior, to whom he need ascribe no aesthetic misgivings, and who does not know the rest of his life and cannot criticize it."[33] A civilized man, Freud affirms, "will indubitably find that at the bottom of his heart he too regards the sexual act as something degrading, which soils and contaminates not only the body."[34] And the origin of this attitude, Freud continues, lies in the fact that during his youth, when sexual passions were already developed, their gratification was almost as completely prohibited outside the family as within it. Women's frigidity, says Freud, like men's impotence, is "the consequence of the long period of delay between sexual maturity and sexual activity which is demanded by education for social reasons."[35]

The alternative of sexual liberty, however, according to Freud, holds out no better hope for the happiness of mankind. Man is defeated whatever he does in his quest for well-being. "Unrestrained sexual liberty from the beginning," Freud writes, "leads to no better result. It is easy to show that the value the mind sets on erotic needs instantly sinks as soon as satisfaction becomes readily obtainable. Some obstacle is necessary to swell the tide of the libido to its height. . . . In times during which no obstacles to sexual satisfaction existed, such as, may be, during the decline of the civilizations of antiquity, love became worthless, life became empty, and strong reaction-formations were necessary before the indispensable emotional values of love could be recovered. In this context it may be stated that

the ascetic tendency of Christianity had the effect of rais-
ing the psychical value of love in a way that heathen antiquity could never achieve. . . ."[36] This then is the dilemma of man's sexual instinct—repressions divide his life,
making him unhappy by their separation of sensuality
from tenderness—liberty, on the other hand, deprives sexuality of the intensity which grows only in the presence of
obstacles. As in Schopenhauer's philosophy, satisfaction
eludes us, deprivation pains us. What shall a liberal ethics
answer to Freud's melancholy reflections?

In the first place, civilization is not an agency which
necessarily sunders sensuality from tenderness. The col-
lection of love lyrics of ancient Palestine, gathered together in *The Song of Songs,* for instance, are remarkable
precisely because of their union between tenderness and
sensuality. Love, in its fullness of sense and affection, was
the experience of the land's ordinary people. The songs
were expressions of folk emotions. "They voice the joy
felt by the young on the awakening of passionate love; and
the popularity which the songs must have enjoyed and
which led to their preservation was due to the response
that they found in the hearts of those who heard them and
sang them."[37] Physical passion and tenderness can be conjoined in a love which is untainted by the excremental
associations of evil which haunt Freud. The delight which
lovers take in each other in *The Song of Songs* extends to
all their organs and all their smells. This is love without
the dark guilt which pervades Freud's account, and which
evoked Bernard Shaw's judgment that the Bible's "one
great love poem is the only one that can satisfy a man who
is really in love. Shelley's Epipsychidion is, in comparison
literary gas and gaiters."[38]

There is no suggestion in *The Song of Songs* of the
need for an ethically inferior object with whom there will

be no aesthetic misgivings or cultural restraints. Instead, the lovers boast of each other and themselves with complete naturalness.

The influences which separate the affectionate from the sensual in man, furthermore, are not inherent in the notion of culture itself. Restrictions on incest become an acute problem for the adolescent only when cultural forces tend to establish an over-intense relationship between mother and son. The inequality of men and women is especially a causal factor in the Oedipus Complex formation, and its subsequent effect on later sexual life. A society of patriarchal dominance breeds the Oedipus Complex as a form of compensatory sexual relationship. A wife who as an unequal is unhappy in her sexual relations, a wife who is not in love with her husband, and who may have had no choice in her marriage, tends to cultivate an especial sexual tie with her son; he becomes, as it were, a kind of surrogate lover. The patterns of marital discontent and rebellion against restrictions on incest are thus interrelated with the social inequality of men and women. Something of this sort seems to have been the case in the home environment of Freud as a child. His young and pretty mother was the second wife of a middle-aged man who already had a grandchild; Freud brooded over his father's rebuffs, and took solace in his mother's strong attachment. The love of a son perhaps fulfilled to some extent a young woman's longing for a youthful lover.

Incest restrictions, of themselves, do not seem to place a great strain upon the human personality. Indeed, their basis seems to be much more in the biological workings of the sexual drive than Freud would concede. Sexual impulse is tied to adventure; the familiar, the oft-seen, fails to rouse sexual energies. Abundant experience confirms Westermarck's judgment that the fundamental cause of exogamy is the sexual indifference which arises among those who have lived in close association.[39] The restrictions on incest give rise to difficulties only under special social circumstances. A young wife, thwarted in her sexual impulses, will draw emotional consolation from her son. Where such social circumstances are widespread, there is an indication that the structure of the family and the institution of marriage require the attention of social science. But there is no insuperable problem which a destiny of incest raises to baffle the efforts for a liberal civilization.

The long postponement of sexual experience and marriage is likewise a cultural situation which a liberal society can reconstruct. A long delay between sexual maturity and sexual activity is not a necessity of civilization, and Freud's observation on this point, accurate perhaps for his own Viennese middle class setting of the late nineteenth century, is much less valid for contemporary American society. The movements of sexual education, moreover, have changed the attitudes of people in significant respects. The "well-brought-up wife" is now judged by canons other than those of Freud's time; upbringing is not now synonymous with sexual ignorance. The wife today has generally read with some care into the questions of sexual satisfaction, sexual experience is not regarded as degrading, and it is common knowledge that there has been a recession in men's emotional need for "less exalted sexual objects."

Freud, however, believes that the sexual ethics of a liberal society is also foredoomed to bring unhappiness. He believes, as we have seen, that sexual passion requires the incitement of obstacles. A liberal sexual ethics, however, does not abrogate the biological basis of love; courtship itself, the slower response of woman, imposes a sufficient biological obstacle for the lover. Superimposed barriers are not required to awaken or heighten love. The heritage of ancient taboos has produced the association of sexual love with forbidden fruit; the rebellious taking of delight in that which authority has forbidden becomes a kind of false end-in-itself which commingles with sexual experience. That which is forbidden is regarded as the more enjoyable. But taboos and social repressions thereby contaminate sexual joy with the impulses of aggression and hatred; the acts of love are then suffused with the angry spirit of defiance, with rebellion against social codes and the super-ego, and the sexual partner is an instrument of this aggression. Until love recovers its own character, free from such admixtures, the potentialities of human happiness will have been far from realized. The anchorite Paphnutius may have been lashed by obstacles into a fury of desire for Thaïs, but the intensity of feeling was compounded of much besides the component of love; there was hatred, rebellion, the accumulated anger of frustration.

Life became empty in the decline of civilizations because the human affections had been disturbed. Systems of slavery, political repression, organized cruelty, the fears of superstition, had deprived men of their capacities for simple joy and friendliness. The sexual licence of the upper classes was not sexual freedom; it was not the joyful experience of freemen, but their channel of aggression and ego-enhancement. And the ascetic tendency of Christianity did not raise the psychical value of love. The repressions of the Middle Ages subdued people, and weakened their emotional drives. Perhaps there has lingered in Freud's theory something of the self-hatred which was inculcated by the Platonic-Christian tradition. For in his doctrine, too, the biological drives are pre-judged to culminate in defeat; the foundations of emotional life are undermined by the knowledge that unhappiness is its necessary conclusion. A projective metaphysics of despair hovers over all the springs of feeling.

8. The Advancement of Civilization as the Increase of Human Happiness

In three respects, especially, has the advancement of civilization increased the sexual happiness of people. The replacement of polygamy with monogamy made possible a more widespread instinctual satisfaction; secondly, the recognition of romantic love, which became prevalent with the Industrial Revolution, liberated personal choices in sexual experience; and lastly, the modern feminist movement, with its egalitarian spirit, brought a marked concern for the sexual well-being of women.

It may seem to contravene common sense when we assert that the change from polygamy to monogamy has made for increased sexual contentment. One tends, like Freud, to think of the possible sexual mates who are unavailable. Polygamy, however, as an historic institution, has meant wives for the few, and abstinence for the many. Solomon with his thousand wives and concubines must have condemned many men to a wifeless status. The story of David and Bathsheba may be regarded as a document of social criticism directed against polygamy. The monopoly of women by the rich was at the expense of the deprived poor. Nathan the prophet denounced David who had taken for himself the wife of another man. David, said the prophet, was like a rich man, with many sheep and cattle, who had dispossessed a poor man of his single lamb. "Thou art the man!" the prophet thundered. Under usual conditions, monogamy is an effective instrument for distributing sexual satisfactions to almost the whole population, something which polygamy fails to do. If we recognize that hitherto the choice for the many has been between abstinence or monogamy, we will acknowledge that the achievement of civilization in this respect has been considerable. Civilization has diminished a primary source of sexual frustration.

Even in modern times, of course, special circumstances have induced a recurrence of polygamy. The polygamy of the Mormons was attractive to many women on the American Eastern seaboard because migrations to the frontier were depleting their communities of marriageable young men. The era of westward expansion was also that of the New England spinster. Polygamy was practised by the Mormons in an almost self-denying, Puritan spirit, to bring sexual satisfaction to those who had lacked the allure to win a husband.[40] The social conditions which promoted this institution, were, however, exceptional. Whatever modifications may now emerge in the institution of marriage in the process of civilization, one may surmise that they will not be in the direction of the traditional polygamy with its system of enforced frustration.

The individual choice of one's husband or wife which became accepted in modern civilization meant a freer sexual expression. The poetry of love, the experienced awakening of the fresh intensity of emotions, became part of European civilization. The stilted lady of repression, whom medieval chronicles had celebrated, is set aside with bygone artificialities. The novels of the eighteenth century, with their discovery of the adventures of an individual hero, and the literature of feeling and nature which swept through Europe in the early nineteenth century, marked the decline of repressive values, the abnegation of desires. With spontaneity and self-expression in emotional life, sexual experience was no longer embittered by the consciousness that one's innermost choices had been violated.

Meanwhile, women like Mary Wollstonecraft initiated the movement for the liberation of their sex. The dominant opinion of mankind has set narrow confines to the possible happiness of one-half its members. And contemporary thought, despite official disclaimers, is still considerably moulded by this standpoint. Freud's philosophy on the place of women plainly sets forth a socio-biological pessimism. "Nature," he says, "has paid less careful attention to the demands of the female function than to those of masculinity."[41] Woman, he holds, is biologically inclined toward passive aims; she is masochist in spirit, and needs to be loved more than to love. Her anatomical structure, moreover, makes her forever envious of man. Women, he concludes, have contributed little to the discoveries and inventions of civilization; perhaps, says Freud, they did discover the technical process of plaiting and weaving. "If this is so, one is tempted to guess at the unconscious motive at the back of this achievement."[42]

Freud's woman is Nora before she has emerged from *A Doll's House*. The Central European *hausfrau* seems to have sat for her portrait in Freud's psychology; she is depicted as a passive sexual object, without real capacity for happiness except in her role as mother to her children, an obedient servant to man's welfare, someone who can at best know the joys of a favored concubine. The self-denigration of women is still deeply ingrained in surviving cultures. On the Sabbath observance of the Orthodox Jews, the men intone: "Blessed be God for having made me a man," and the women chant: "Blessed be God for having made me as he chose." The small child listens and wonders at the arbitrary unfairness of this arrangement. Cosmic injustice is then part of God's decree. But why should one thank God for assignment to inferior status? Did Freud as a child learn in his home of the fate which the divine will had conferred upon women? Had he accepted this cosmic edict, as he did social conventions, under protest? In any case, his philosophy averred without qualification that woman's role is that of the passive tool, the submissive instrument.

Mary Wollstonecraft was ridiculed by her contemporaries as a "hyena in petticoats." The ancient morality, which reinforced a passive role on women in sexual life, resisted with violence the suggestion of women's equality with men. The feminist movement, however, in time succeeded in convincing men that much of the so-called passivity of women was the outcome of socially repressive conventions. The myth of the passive woman was the counterpart of the sadistic attitude with which men had involved their own sexual outlook. Men's aggressive impulses could vent themselves in a situation which provided them with a sexual scapegoat, and they demanded a willing acceptance of this role on the part of women. The cruelty of men itself was, in large part, the expression of social frustrations; the inequalities of the social structure, the burdens of resentment, their emotional traumas and wounds, manifested themselves at their ugliest in men's sexual experience. Hence, it was that political economic liberation was followed so soon by the beginnings of the emancipation of women. Freedom overflows; emotions of good-will prevail within one as one's own freedom is realized; the free man needs no slave. It was to revolutionary France, where the rights of man had been pledged, that Mary Wollstonecraft looked for her first vindication of the rights of woman. Those who had overthrown oppression would not feel the need to oppress others.

The stereotype of women's willing passivity began to dissolve. The medical and social sciences in the twentieth century began to discuss frankly the problems of the happiness of women in sexual relations. The literature of love became conspicuous in its contribution to the contemporary arts of living; the tree of knowledge had more fruits than Eve or the serpent had suspected. Women made the self-discovery of themselves as lovers. Woman's status as an equal sexual participant was a major achievement of social revolution, for the mark of inferiority had hitherto been stamped upon her sexual role.

Such then are the achievements of civilization in promoting the sexual happiness of people. Incomplete they may be, but they are enough to confute the notion that civilization is an agency for the frustration of men. Although human societies can be built as systems largely for the repression of men, it is also true that civilizations achieved greatness with their liberation of human energies. This historical possibility is all that free men require. An ethics enlightened by psychoanalysis and the social sciences can contribute to the unfinished business of civilization.

9. Estrangement from Mankind

Freud's theory of civilization must finally be regarded as a species of primitivism, a primitivist philosophy of history. "Cultural primitivism," says the noted scholar Lovejoy, "is the discontent of the civilized with civilization, or with some conspicuous and characteristic feature of it. It is the belief of men living in a relatively highly evolved and complex cultural condition that a life far simpler and less sophisticated in some or in all respects is a more desirable life."[43] Freud believed indeed that instinctual happiness was greater among our pre-historic ancestors than among ourselves. Primitivism denies that progress is possible; it affirms that civilization necessarily brings an increase of frustration and renunciation, but it has no hope that men will desist from their experiment in culture. "Knowledge increaseth sorrow," said Ecclesiastes, and the primitivist awaits with sadness the increase in both.

What are the psychological sources of the primitivist philosophy of history? In its disillusionmemnt with the life of civilization, it projects upon the past the fantasy of a happy Golden Age. Primitivism is associated with a metaphysical vision which would transcend the weary categories of science and reason. The primitivist in history seeks solace in the womb of time; the primitivist in metaphysics wishes surcease from the world of distinct things and separate realities. The primitivist metaphysician seeks the unity and primal peace which were given in his mother's womb; there all distinctions were annihilated, and his personality was embraced within a comforting totality. The "ultimate reality," biological energy, duplicates in Freud's metaphysics the properties of existence in primal maternal absorption. "The laws of logic—above all, the law of contradiction do not hold for processes in the id. . . . There is nothing in the id which can be compared to negation, and we are astonished to find in it an exception to the philosopher's assertion that space and time are necessary forms of our mental acts."[44] A world without separations, a world which transcends the appearances of space-time is the "ultimate being" in Freud's primitivist metaphysics.

The primitivist estrangement from contemporary civilization was, for Freud, largely a response to the phenomenon of war. The first World War brought him a disillusionment not untypical of our time. Only those blind to facts could espouse an optimist philosophy:

"When I speak of disillusionment, everyone at once knows what I mean. . . . We had expected the great ruling powers among the white nations upon whom the leadership of the human species has fallen, who were known to have cultivated world-wide interests, to whose creative powers were due our technical advances in the direction of dominating nature, as well as the artistic and scientific acquisitions of the mind—peoples such as these we had expected to succeed in discovering another way of settling misunderstandings and conflicts of interest. . . . The enjoyment of this fellowship in civilization was from time to time disturbed by warning voices which declared that . . . war was unavoidable, . . . We refused to believe it; but if such a war must be, what was our imaginary picture of it? We saw it as an opportunity for demonstrating the progress of mankind in communal feeling. . . . Then the war in which we had refused to believe broke out, and brought —disillusionment. Not only is it more sanguinary and more destructive than any war of other days . . . ; but it is at least as cruel, as embittered, as implacable as any that preceded it. . . . It rends all bonds of fellowship between the contending peoples, . . . Well may that civilized cosmopolitan of whom I spoke, stand helpless in a world grown strange to him . . ."[45]

Whether civilization can solve the problems of men's hatred and aggression, we cannot say. One thing, however, we do know. The myth of primal primitive happiness will be of no assistance in our contemporary problems; it provides a regressive outlet, a make-believe infantile security, but it does not contribute to the insight or knowledge which is required. The primitivist rejection of civilization proceeds from an ancient tradition; Biblical fantasy depicted the Garden of Eden as a paradise of food-gathering, where happiness and innocence flourished in an age before man was condemned to work by the sweat of his brow. The state of nature in Rousseau's doctrine, the Marxian postulate of primitive communism, are later versions of

primitivist projection. All these myths have much in
common; as items of sociological folklore, each has its
Fall, each has its bearer of guilt. The guilt of Adam is like
that of the primitive capitalist accumulator—each ini-
tiates a Great Lapse. And all the primitivist myths have
shared an anti-intellectualist bias—from Genesis with its
antipathy to the Tree of Knowledge, to Rousseau's apothe-
osis of feeling, and the Marxians' conception of ideology.

The tragedy of Freud is that of the estranged ethical
philosopher, who perceives a vision of human happiness,
but who lives in a world where people seem to choose to
be unhappy. Every civilized man will feel himself partially
alienated from a world in which irrational forces are
dominant. Hence, the great ethical leaders have cursed
the people whom they would have helped, cursed them
for their smallness of mind and poverty of spirit; they
have indeed wished the world to die. Moses flung down
the tablets, and blazed out in anger: "Sword on thigh,
every man of you, and sweep the camp from side to side,
killing all your kinsfolk, your friends, and your fellow-
countrymen." Later prophets have done the same. Bernard
Shaw's tablets were the *Fabian Essays in Socialism,* and
when he saw humanity, in its stupidity, reject the wisdom
of its Saints, he called for the destruction of the human
race as an unsuccessful experiment in Creative Evolution.
"There is no sense in us. We are useless, dangerous, and
ought to be abolished." *Man and Superman* told the same
last words as *Heartbreak House.* Neither peace nor violence would help mankind; both were "fundamentally
futile." "Man will return to his idols and his cupidities, in
spite of all 'movements' and all revolutions, until his nature is changed." The catastrophe of war, said Shaw, "confirmed a doubt which had steadily grown in my mind during my forty years of public work as a Socialist; namely,
whether the human animal, as he exists at present, is

capable of solving the social problems raised by his own aggregation, or, as he calls it, his civilization." What perhaps for Shaw was only one mood among others was the last testament of his great contemporary, H. G. Wells. Wells had devoted a lifetime to the faith that he had imbibed from his teacher, Huxley, that science would save mankind. His novels and histories were a research magnificent dedicated to this faith. Yet as he lay dying, hope was gone out. *Mind at the End of its Tether* he called his last work. "The human story," he wrote, "has already come to an end. . . . There are thousands of mean, perverted, malicious, heedless and cruel individuals coming into daylight every day, resolute to frustrate the kindlier purpose of man."

Extremes meet. Revolutionist, reformer, and psychoanalyst, all have found humanity hateful and wanting, and its civilization a venture into nullity. Love of mankind is transmuted into the opposite. Can we find a basis for action which will not entrap us within the dialectic of estrangement?

Civilization can advance human happiness, but how far, we cannot tell. For perhaps human efforts reach an upper limit, and there may be ineradicable conditions which restrict the possibilities of social reconstruction.

Is there some deep-seated propensity for hatred among men? Is there some instinct or drive toward aggression which is beyond the reach of the social reformer? So much of one's philosophy of mankind depends upon the answer to this question, but here again, what knowledge we have merges into an indeterminate area.

In 1932, as signs were multiplying that war and hatred would break forth with new immensity upon the world, Albert Einstein wrote a plea to Freud that he bring to bear his far-reaching knowledge of man's instinctive life upon this problem. It seemed to Einstein that there was a "lust for hatred and destruction" in man, which under unusual circumstances took on the proportions of a collective neurosis. What could be done to help man overcome the propensity toward hatred?

Freud's reply was a melancholy one. He could see "no likelihood of our being able to suppress humanity's aggressive tendencies." The atrocities recorded in human history seemed to him to show that "the ideal motive has often served as a camouflage for the lust of destruction." Man, Freud believed, is driven by a death instinct, which can become an impulse toward destruction when it is directed toward external objects; but this death instinct, he said, is part of man's original, uneliminable nature. He had read the tales of anthropologists about happy, peaceful peoples who dwelled in distant isles; he thought they were fairy tales, written in the language of social science. "This I can hardly credit; I would like further details about these happy folk."[46] Perhaps one might try to divert man's aggressive tendencies to other channels, but Freud believed this would upset the sexual well-being of man. Civilization might develop ideals of social affection, but the unstable equilibrium between civilization and hatred would remain. One could never foresee upon what occasion calamity would break forth to rend the thin garment of culture. Then all of men's brutish forces would assert themselves with violence.

A less pessimistic school of psychologists has refused, however, to concede that hatred and aggression are innate in men. They have defended the hypothesis that aggression is always the consequence of frustration; where aggressive behavior occurs, they say, it springs from some situation of frustration, and conversely, where frustration exists, it will give rise to some mode of aggression. The frustration-aggression hypothesis has a unique applicability to social problems. There was, for instance, a high correlation in fourteen Southern states, during the years from 1882 to 1930, between the number of lynchings and the annual per acre value of cotton.[47] With adverse economic conditions, in other words, the number of lynchings tended to rise. There were more frustrations of goal responses in times of economic difficulty, and this expressed itself in an increase in the regional form of aggressive action. The frustration-aggression hypothesis is consistent with great social hopes.[48] If men's hatreds are all the outcome of social frustrations, then, if a society were reconstructed to eliminate the sources of frustration, wars and hatreds would disappear.

But is this hypothesis true? To what extent is it verifiable? There is abundant evidence that a correlation exists between frustration and aggression, but how extensive is the domain of the correlation? If frustration were reduced to near zero, would aggressive impulses tend likewise to vanish? Or is there an irreducible quantum of aggressive drive, which is the minimal limit to any decrease in aggressive behavior? If such is the case, we should have a broad domain of life-situations in which diminished frustration would involve a corresponding diminution of aggressive response. But the equation would have a deceptive structure. For in its lower reaches, one would enter within a region in which reduced frustrations would fail to affect the hard core of uneliminable aggressive behavior. Indeed, the operations of an irreducible aggressive tendency would lead persons to create situations of frustration; the person who feels aggressive can always look for some situation which "frustrates" him. "Frustrations" would then be rationalized occasions in satisfaction for aggression. A kind of pseudo-correlation between "frustration" and aggression would obtain. For, it would not be an experienced frustration which would have initiated an aggressive response. Rather the person's experienced amorphous aggression would have prompted him to find some hitherto tranquil situation to constitute a frustration; the "frustration" would be the scapegoat for a basic aggressive propensity.

The grounds of evolutionary biology make it plausible that some irreducible fund of aggressive impulse exists. Those individuals thus endowed would have had, perhaps, a greater chance of survival than their peacefully inclined fellows. The selective process of the struggle for existence may have sifted out for man a biological inheritance which included a basic aggressive drive. The evil in man which preoccupies theology would then simply be the fact of his biological descent. There is an amazing similarity between the neo-Calvinist theology of Reinhold Niebuhr and the evolutionary theory of Julian Huxley. The biologist writes: "The microcosm of the individual personality incorporates by inescapable heredity, a swarm of impulses, many of them astonishingly bad and violent. Indeed it is only the helplessness of the infant which prevents us from realizing the extent and strength of the evil which it contains, and it has needed the learned labours of analytic psychology to reveal the amount of badness with which every human nature has to cope during his or her development. The 'original evil' is part of what theologians call original sin . . ."[49]

How then shall we decide between the two rival hypotheses concerning the status of man's aggressive behavior? At the crucial domain of dispute, our means of verification lapse. To test these hypotheses in the range where frustrations are near zero, we should have to produce organisms in whom frustrations were nearly absent; the absence of aggressive behavior would then be decisive evidence. But no such creatures can be exhibited. Every child is born powerless, moving in a world it does not comprehend to satisfy its needs, crying, kicking, grasping, regurgitating.

The powerlessness of the child is itself a decree of frustration. And every process of birth is likewise one of traumatic frustration. With pressures on its skull and body, gasping with deprivation of oxygen, choking and struggling desperately, the infant life starts with frustration and struggle. The frustrationless organism is like a psychological absolute zero; our extrapolations of what is or is not true in that domain are inevitably speculative. And if an irreducible quantum of aggressive tendency will always associate with itself some situation of frustration, if biological tendency itself creates its "reasons" and occasions for hostility, then our efforts at verifying one of our theories by some crucial experiment are defeated. We cannot with the present resources of psychological science, presume to a complete answer to the question of man's original nature.

There is a hope, however, for the happiness of mankind. Whatever the ultimate nature of man may be we can undertake a practicable human task—to reduce the sources of known frustrations. Because we are men, it is the only foundation upon which we can work, the postulate we give to our social action. Perhaps the hope is frail, but history has not written a negative decree, and human effort, surmounting the past, may achieve the vision and reality of a life liberated from hatred and fear.

References

1. Freud, Sigmund: *Civilization and Its Discontents*, transl. by Joan Riviere. London, Hogarth Press, 1930, p. 123.
2. *Ibid.*, p. 63.
3. *Ibid.*, p. 74.
4. *Ibid.*, p. 75-76.
5. *Ibid.*, p. 120-121.
6. *Ibid.*, p. 102.
7. *Ibid.*, p. 91.
8. Turberville, A. S.: *English Men and Manners in the Eighteenth Century*. Oxford, Clarendon Press, 1929, p. 4-6.

9. Huizinga, J.: *The Waning of the Middle Ages*, transl. by F. Hopman. London, Arnold, 1924, p. 22.

10. The Confucian doctrine of filial piety, it has been observed, "was preached to an age where parricide was not uncommon." Fitzgerald, C. P.: *China*. New York, Appleton, 1938, p. 87.

11. Koch, G. Adolf: *Republican Religion: The American Revolution and the Cult of Reason*. New York, Columbia Univ. Press, 1933, p. 32-33, 61, 242, 286-287.

12. Chinard, Gilbert: *Thomas Jefferson*. Boston, Little, 1929, p. 75.

13. *The Writings of Thomas Jefferson*, Monticello Edition, Vol. XV. edited by Andrew A. Lipscomb, Washington, Thomas Jefferson Memorial Association, 1904, p. 219.

14. Webb, Beatrice: *My Apprenticeship*, Vol. I. London, Penguin, 1938, p. 204-209.

15. Kropotkin, Peter: *Memoirs of a Revolutionist*. Boston, Houghton, 1899, p. 301-302.

16. Freud, Sigmund: *Civilization and Its Discontents*. Loc. cit., p. 127.

17. Kropotkin, Prince: *Ethics: Origin and Development*, transl. by Louis S. Friedland and Joseph R. Piroshnikoff. New York, Dial Press, 1924, p. 245.

18. *The Bible*, translated by James Moffatt. New York, Harper, 1935, p. 4.

19. A related line of reasoning is found in Rieff, Philip: The meaning of history and religion in Freud's thought. *J. Religion, XXXI:*127-128, 1951.

20. Frazer, J. G.: *The Golden Bough, The Magic Art and the Evolution of Kings*, Vol. II. London, Macmillan, 1911, p. 118.

21. de Spinoza, Benedict: *Short Treatise on God, Man, and His Well-being*, transl. and edited by A. Wolf. London, Black, 1910, p. 133.

22. Freud, Sigmund: *Collected Papers*, Vol. 4, 3rd Ed., transl. by Joan Riviere. London, Hogarth Press, 1946, p. 215.

23. Style, Jane M.: *Auguste Comte: Thinker and Lover*. London, Trench, Trubner, 1928, p. 86.

24. Freud, Sigmund: *Civilization and Its Discontents*. Loc. cit., p. 79-80.

25. Harris, Frank: *Bernard Shaw*. New York, Simon & Schuster, Inc., 1931, p. 224.

26. Rostovtzeff, Michael I.: *Mystic Italy*. New York, Holt, 1927, p. 7.

27. Klausner, Joseph: *From Jesus to Paul*, transl. by William F. Stinespring. New York, Macmillan, 1943.

28. *First Epistle to the Corinthians,* 3:16. *Epistle to the Romans,* 8:13, 7:18.

29. Dollard, John: *Caste and Class in a Southern Town*. New Haven, Yale, 1937, p. 399, 416, 430, 384.

30. Cf., especially, Kardiner, Abram, and Ovesey, Lionel: *The Mark of Oppression*. New York, Norton, 1951, p. 69-70, 85-87, 97, 118, 290. Also, cf., Frazier, E. Franklin: *The Negro in the United States*. New York, Macmillan, 1949, p. 318.

31. Freud, Sigmund: *Collected Papers,* Vol. 4. *Loc. cit.,* p. 214.
32. *Ibid.,* p. 207.
33. *Ibid.,* p. 210.
34. *Ibid.,* p. 211.
35. *Ibid.,* p. 212.
36. *Ibid.,* p. 213.
37. Jastrow, Morris, Jr.: *The Song of Songs,* Philadelphia, Lippincott, 1921, p. 12.
38. Shaw, Bernard: *The Adventures of the Black Girl in Her Search for God.* London, Constable, 1932, p. 67.
39. Westermarck, Edward: *The History of Human Marriage,* Vol. II, 5th Ed. New York, Allerton, 1922, p. 192.
40. Werner, M. R.: *Brigham Young.* New York, Harcourt, 1925, p. 300.
41. Freud, Sigmund: *New Introductory Lectures. Loc. cit.,* p. 180.
42. *Ibid.,* p. 157-158, 180, 181.
43. Lovejoy, Arthur O., and Boas, George: *Primitivism and Related Ideas in Antiquity.* Baltimore, Johns Hopkins Press, 1935, p. 7.
44. Freud, Sigmund: *New Introductory Lectures on Psychoanalysis, Loc. cit.,* p. 104.
45. Freud, Sigmund: Thoughts for the times on war and death, in *Collected Papers,* Vol. IV. *Loc. cit.,* p. 289-294.
46. Einstein, Albert, and Freud, Sigmund: *Why War?* International Institute of Intellectual Cooperation, League of Nations, 1933, p. 18, 44-47.
47. Dollard, John, and associates: *Frustration and Aggression.* New Haven, Yale, 1939, p. 1-31.
48. Malinowski, Bronislaw: An anthropological analysis of war, in Malinowski, Bronislaw: *Magic, Science, and Religion.* Boston, Beacon Press, 1948, p. 282-283.
49. Huxley, Julian: *Touchstone for Ethics. Loc. cit.,* p. 226.

PART THREE

FINAL QUESTIONS

1. The Self-doubt of Cultural Relativity

THE SELF-DOUBT of contemporary society has taken on the character of a neurosis. The scepticism of liberal thinkers has corroded the foundations of their own ethics.

Social scientists find themselves as personalities sundered in two. As human individuals, they are loyal to liberal values; in their professional capacity, however, they must hold these values to be arbitrary and irrational. Ruth Benedict, a sensitive person, affirmed for instance, that all cultures are incommensurable. Her philosophy of cultural relativity became dominant among American social scientists. According to this doctrine, each culture is as valid as any other; each culture is a self-consistent pattern of thought and action. Every society is believed to be a "whole" in which component institutions are integrated, and the "organic unities" of other peoples are to be revered. Cultural relativity is conjoined with a principle of ethical relativity; it holds that there is no trans-cultural criticism of basic value-postulates.

Cultural relativity entails, however, that all ethical criticism is a soliloquy within one's cultural universe. The liberal cannot then pretend to criticize the authoritarian; each is confined to his respective incommensurable world.

At first, the doctrine of cultural relativity commended itself to liberals as consonant with their anti-imperialist feeling. Ethnocentrism is the cultural core of imperialism, for the imperialist presumes to assert that his culture is superior to others, that his way of life is more grounded in the nature of "reality" than others. Anthropological wisdom, as spoken by Ruth Benedict, rejected the imperialist ideology, and bade men be tolerant toward the divergences of other cultures.[1]

What the cultural relativist fails, however, to perceive, is that *no* ethical consequence follows from the anthropological fact of cultural variation. No ethical imperative of tolerance for other cultural ways follows from the discovery of their diversity. If intolerance is part of your cultural pattern, if you regard intolerance as a basic value, then by your doctrine of cultural relativity, you are immune to criticism. For intolerance is then a component of your cultural whole, integral to your way of life, and he who advises you to abandon intolerance is trying to impose upon you an alien cultural value. If lynching is part of certain regional folkways, then it is presumed defensible simply by virtue of that fact. An intolerant community will have no difficulty in denying the precept "judge not, that ye be not judged," because its moral code, no matter what we think, is its own validation.

Cultural relativity began with a deep sympathy for the values of peoples, especially the weak, primitive ones. Faithful observers had recorded how imperialism uprooted primitive communal values even as it did their economies. Cultural relativity was a protest against the smug moral complacency which was the counterpart of economic imperialism; it condemned the moral imperialist. But cultural relativity itself denied a common humanity; it found no values universal in men. And its own doctrine therefore could provide the apology for "values" of cruelty and hatred which claimed a cultural immunity from all criticism.

A philosophical dogma cannot easily repress the assertion of universal human values. The standards of common

humanity break through the pages of the committed
cultural relativist. Ruth Benedict, for instance, found
that certain cultures were "genuinely disoriented," beset
by a "conflict of disharmonious elements." She meditated
the wasteful tensions which competitive society engenders,
and her criterion of evaluation was human frustration and
satisfaction.[2] Margaret Mead warns against using "cross-
cultural data"; she holds that value-systems are integral to
their respective cultures, and doubts that there is a trans-
cultural standard of evaluation. But the same scientist tells
us that we have much to learn from the Samoans.[3] Our
tiny, ingrown family, Margaret Mead says, makes for
crippling attitudes of dependence and neurotic relationships which are avoided by the larger family community
in Samoa. In practice, she assumes a criterion of universal
human values common to all cultures. The consistent
ethical relativist would be unable to speak of the "dishar-
mony" of other cultural wholes; he would have to classify
such judgments of his own as scientifically meaningless
asides. But the aside, the *obiter dictum,* sheds a light upon
the underlying philosophy, a truer perception of the
person's philosophy than the formal statements for public
consumption.

The universal ethics, which is the outcome of psychoanalysis, rests on the scientific belief that there is a common biological foundation in all the branches of the
human race. Psychoanalysis confirms the basis for ethical
universalism, and therefore can guide, without inconsist-
ency, the efforts of applied anthropology. The great contemporary programs of technical aid and medical assistance
to the world's backward areas are founded on such a common ethical philosophy. Frustrations and satisfactions are
the criterion by which cultural forms are evaluated; the
common biological basis is the validation of the psycho-

analysis of cultural values. The suffering which a given cultural value engenders is an indication that an underlying biological drive has been frustrated by the given cultural form. Cultural institutions differ in the extent to which they achieve the satisfaction of biological drives. Each society has its characteristic satisfactions and frustrations. Some cultures are exceedingly repressive of human drives, others have achieved a higher degree of expression. The repressive cultures are those whose social forms have produced intense human suffering. The free society is that set of social institutions which promote the maximum expressions and the minimum repressions, the free society is the ideal of the highest practicable level of human happiness.

A common ideal for humanity is meaningful only because it is founded on laws of psychology common to all human beings. If ethical relativity were true, each cultural universe would have its own distinctive, irreducible laws of psychology, and there would be no general laws common to all cultures.[4] There would be power-seekers, wealth-seekers, self-abnegators, but there would not be men. The basic needs and drives, however, are common to all men; that is why there are no incommensurable cultural universes. Each culture is a group of learned modes of behavior, each culture is constituted by a network of responses to material and social stimuli. Underlying all cultures are universal laws of stimulus and response, and each culture may be regarded as a special case of the operations of these laws under defined social and geographical circumstances. The diversity of cultural forms reflects differences in historical conditioning, differences in the directions which institutions give to persons. The child is born tradition-less; alternative routes of conditioning channelize the child's drives into different cultural expressions, but a common biological humanity is shared beneath all the cultural divergences. Traditions are woven into the child's life by the use of conditioning mechanisms which conform to universal law. Cultural configurations are not unique, unanalyzable totalities. Every culture is a defined instance of the laws of individual psychology. Cultures are not immune to analysis, and the doctrine that they are is, indeed, a kind of resistance to the analyst's work. And where a culture has become confused, bewildered, where it is haunted by fear and guilt, where it is led not by rational insight but by the unknown strains and traumas of its unconscious, psychoanalysis provides the scientific instrument in the quest for clarity and the liberation of action.

The psychoanalytical faith in the existence of universal drives and laws common to all cultures is part of the scientific faith in the existence of general laws. The Aristotelian scholastics held that the laws which governed the admirable celestial entities must be different from those which describe objects on the earth. They maintained that there were incommensurable physical universes; in the heavens, objects moved in perfect eternal circles, whereas on the lowly earth, they travelled in straight lines. It was Newton's vision to look for laws of motion which would apply both to heavenly and terrestrial bodies. Cultural relativity is like the pre-Newtonian scholastic doctrine, whereas the basis for psychoanalysis is the conviction that universal laws of man underlie the diversity of cultures.

The basic values are those with which the person is biologically endowed; they are not the product of social tradition. No value is ultimate if it must be instilled into the person through a process of conditioning. Authentic cultural values are those which promote the maximal satisfaction of the underlying biological drives; they are an expression of the individual's own choices based on an awareness of his basic desires. Inauthentic cultural values eventuate in the repression of underlying drives, and are the outcome not of the individual's own choice but of anxieties which have been embedded in his unconscious. No system of cultural values is endowed with the pre-eminence of an absolute. Every system of cultural values is open to the self-revision which comes with the complete consciousness as to whether these values are authentically one's own, and the process of self-evaluation affirms the ultimate criterion of human happiness.

Nietzsche sought for a transvaluation of values because he reacted from the morality of slavish masochist self-hatred to the morality of the master's sadism. Contemporary philosophers have contrived an academic analysis which culminates in a devaluation of values; they achieve a self-destructive consummation in asserting that they have nothing to say. Psychoanalysis and the social sciences, by probing into the innermost sources of men's values, help them to recover their freedom, they help them to find their own authentic values. Not transvaluation, not devaluation, but man's own valuation. That is the contribution which the human sciences can make toward the free society.

2. Ultimate Uncertainty

The road which we have taken was chosen on the basis of one simple belief. We have assumed that knowledge and understanding can bring wisdom and happiness to people. Yet here it must be confessed we are at once brought to an ultimate uncertainty. There was the ancient tradition of Ecclesiastes which said: "Knowledge increaseth sorrow." There is, on the other hand, the modern creed of Bacon: "Knowledge is power." The axiom of psychological inquiry is that Socrates spoke well when he said "Know thyself." Self-knowledge, the elimination of the unconscious, the bringing of all to the clarity of consciousness, unflinch-

ing honesty toward one's self—this is the foundation for
the new science and ethics of man. Repressed memories,
repressed hatreds, projective tendencies, all these are to be
brought forth from their hiding-place. Repression is a
sort of dishonesty which the new scientific conscience for-
bids.

But, precisely at this point, a challenge arises to the
wisdom of science. What if repression and projection per-
form a valid biological function? The oyster spins a protective layer around a particle it cannot ingest; its pearl is
a series of protective surfaces. What if there are certain
realities which our minds cannot genuinely face? What if
there are facts which are unmindable as certain substances
are indigestible? When young scientists rend philosophic
ideas, and depict them as myths, are they motivated by a
desire for human happiness, or by some scientific super-
ego? And the scientific super-ego, the veneration of scientific method, can be just as much the instrument of vin-
dictive cruelty as some superstitious creed.

Is illusion a necessary safeguard for the biological happiness of man? A thoughtful woman once said that every life
is founded upon an illusion, that otherwise life would be
without dramatic significance, and seen for the drab,
dreary affair it really is. What was the role of illusion in
the evolutionary process? We can imagine consciousness,
mentality, as it first emerged in biological evolution. This
mentality was a wonderful thing. It enabled the organism
to survive under the most changing circumstances. It was
a remarkable contrivance. But there are by-products to
every invention. The mentality that contributes to survival
in the struggle with the environment is also capable of
standing outside itself, of regarding life and environment
in their broadest perspectives. If mentality had been confined to its function in solving trial-and-error problems in
the immediate environment, if memories had been re-

stricted to near intervals, if anticipations and expectations never had leaped beyond the next presents, then mentality would have been solely a pragmatic, biological instrument. But mentality also brought wide horizons which exceeded man's survival requirements. It brought a conception of death, of the self, and the universe. And knowledge, which emerged as the instrumentality of life, was perverted in its function so that philosophy became for Plato the study of death.

Each human consciousness in our time has to house a world of cruelties and hatreds, of destroyed children, unrealized love, of the broken aged, a world where social relations often are like diplomatic manoeuvres in an armed truce, the world of the concentration camp and crematorium. An orthodox Rabbi in Israel once told me how he had scanned the historic process in his search for God. He believed that he saw God's hand in the victory of the Israeli armies in the war of their liberation. But he had also pondered the mystery of the six million Jews who were burned and gassed. What divine purpose had been served? He had read Toynbee for an answer, but confessed that he still had none. Can anything but some mode of illusion, repression, or projection make these facts compatible with the activities of ordinary life? Would existence otherwise be livable? We can be moved by one dying child, one man in a crucified agony, but six millions overwhelm and insensitize our consciousness. The animal in the acoustics laboratory becomes deaf to a sound which is prolonged. Thus we become emotionally deaf to a repeated stimulus of horror. We repress the six million asphyxiations, forget the deaths which had no onlookers, those who died without disciples, without a comforting mission; we prefer to forget those who knew death, crude, blunt, as it is on an off-stage setting, when it conspires against all dignity and humanity. Shall we say that some myth of redemption would enable us to live with these facts more easily—the mind's necessary cushion against the unassimilable? Shall we say that the psychoanalyst who destroys illusions has overestimated the capacity of the human mind to confront realities?

Freud was an enemy of illusions. He raised up the reality-principle against the pleasure-principle. Science is the outcome of the first, and opposed to the second. But is the "pleasure principle" itself an indispensable device for enabling human minds to adjust to basic realities? Is it like a protective dam which prevents realities from overwhelming us with a blind, tyrannous flood? Freud's faith was that he was engaged in a reclamation work, like the draining of the Zuyder Zee. He simply assumed that the organism always gains when the contents of the unconscious are brought forward into the clarity of consciousness. But the basic question remains unanswered. Is the unconscious a device which emerged in man's evolution to enable him to live with realities whose conscious recognition might overwhelm him? Are repression and projection aspects of mental functioning which are indispensable? Would we lose an important means for adjustment if we supplanted the unconscious completely with consciousness? Even drainage can be uneconomic, and there are crops which flourish only in flooded soils.

If consciousness emerged as the instrumentality for the solving of problems, perhaps the unconscious arose as the biological expedient for housing unsolved and insoluble problems. When things to be done add up, one can't allow one's self to be held up by an unsolved problem or anxiety. The unconscious is the biological device for putting something out of mind, and getting on with the immediate pressing task. The unsolved problems of the past and insoluble ones of the present are sealed away in the unconscious. For the emergence of mentality was accompanied by no guarantee that every problem would be soluble; the insoluble problems that arose as human by-products may require a final appeal to repression. Thus, perhaps, the unconscious is a biological device which ensures the efficient allocation of energies.

We cannot be certain whether our constant analyses, dissection of myths, our bringing projective motivations to light, are altogether in the interest of men's happiness. Perhaps it makes men happier if they retain as an anodyne some philosophy of history which puts doubts to rest. Philosophies are answers to basic, irremovable anxieties like those of death which obtain in all societies. Are these anxieties made the more difficult by the scientific criticism of consolatory myths? Are we once more overestimating the rational powers of man, overlooking the sorrow and depression which understanding may bring? Are we tampering with a safety-valve with which nature has kindly provided us? Again, we can speak with no assurance.

Perhaps the knowledge that probes beyond workaday difficulties may indeed increase sorrow. But we cannot give up the effort to know and understand. Whether the struggle for self-knowledge may finally bring unhappiness to men, we cannot tell. But once knowledge is upon us, we cannot surrender it. No more than a man can put from his mind by will the image of a beautiful woman he loves. She may lead him into unhappiness, darken his days. But as men, we have no alternative but to follow upon that path, without illusions, knowing that if the minded realities overwhelm us, we cannot live knowingly with illusions, and respect ourselves. When man ate of the Tree of Knowledge, he also discovered his Ignorance. But he cannot undo his choice, and thrust his consciousness from himself without ceasing to live what he values in himself.

The basic questions in an age of choice are unanswer-

able. It is folly to try to repress them. Rather we should
reduce human conflict and cruelty by bringing to light
the submerged personality which lies beneath ideologies
and philosophies. Repressed questions then come into
view, doubts become articulate. Answers will still elude
us. But, in our time, it will have been the highest honesty
and achievement to have questioned. For questioning
brings liberation from false values, and brings the personality to an awareness of its own values. The ultimate
knowledge of history and existence may be denied us, but
we can at least discover our own selves and affirm our own
values, even if their realization will be denied. History and
existence may crush our values, but we shall not venerate
them for their power; we shall not make history our judge.

3. Beyond Ideology

A man without an ideology is today as rare as a man
without a country, and certainly as unrespectable. Modern
history is a history of warring creeds, of passionate faiths,
and the man without an ideology is bannerless in an age
when thinking is enlisted in battalions.

But the upshot of our analysis is that free thought and
action are also free from ideology. What are ideologies?
They are indeed works of presumption. An ideology projects wish-fulfillments where knowledge is unavailable; it
denies those realities whose existence it would repress, it
enhances into ultimates what it prizes. An ideology is a
world-system based on one's political and social feelings,
an attempt, conscious or unconscious, to impose one's
political will upon the nature of the universe. It entangles
emotions, actions, and ideas into one amalgam, so that one
does not know where the emotion ends and the idea begins; it regards every idea as a plan for action, and every
idea as the projection of some interest. The Universe is
handed a card of membership in a political party or affil-

iation to a religious sect; it is declared pluralistic or democratic, dialectical, or organismic.

An age of ideology may finally make men restless with an aspiration for intellectual freedom. They perceive that they have deified words and formulas. Emotions of goodwill, suppressed longings for friendliness, work havoc with the rigidities of ideology.

The age of religious wars was followed by an age of scepticism. The rumor spread through France that there was a king to whom men's religions didn't matter; the sceptic Montaigne was heard asking other men as he asked of himself: "What do I know?" and avowing to an "ignorance, strong and noble, which yields nothing to knowledge in honor and courage—an ignorance which requires as much knowledge to attain as knowledge does itself." The age of fanaticism in England was followed by the age of David Hume. "Enthusiasms" were distrusted, men became modest in their pretensions, and forebore from claims of knowing the universe. With their recognition of their status as men, they became reluctant to immolate themselves upon man-made creeds which were presented as divine-given truths. Men, to act as men, would acknowledge their character, their mixture of ignorance and knowledge.

The adherent to ideology believes that the making of history is its handmaiden. He demands for himself and his followers the assurance that "history is on our side." Ideology makes men believe that they are acting with the blessing, with the sanction of the Total Universe. Cromwell believed he was the servant of the Lord, and executant of His Will upon earth. The Nazi leader, Hitler, saw his political party as fortified by a Weltanschauung; therein was its superiority to liberalism, the weapon which would enable it to battle Marxist ideology on equal terms; ideology brought the assurance that the genocide of the

Jews was "the Lord's work."[5] The communist has the guarantee of ideology that he is of the vanguard of the World Dialectic. All the modes of ideology have a common source of emotional satisfaction. They confer a father's blessing, the approval of a super-ego, when one is feeling most insecure. The ideological fanatic is repressing tremendous segments of his personality; he represses doubts and fears, he inhibits his emotions of good-will, he drives his affections along paths approved by party authority. Emotions of friendship in his life dissolve into nothingness, in his actions he no longer has the sense of freedom. The follower of ideology is always ambivalent toward his church or party, hating it for the way it warps his life, so that he no longer reacts as himself, freshly and spontaneously, but always as the representative, a moment, of historical forces. Cruelty as a political value is the counterpart of an extreme personal repression, and it constructs its own new conscience; the intensified motive for cruelty is internalized as the mandate of the historical super-ego. Ideology gives to the cruelty-dominated man the approval of a cosmic conscience; organized cruelty thus has its unchallengeable certitude of world-historical process. Ideology thus helps provide the internal energy for the repression of humane impulses, and external energy for aggression against others. Ideology is the instrument whereby men repress their human responses, and shape their behavior to a political mandate.

Liberal civilization begins when the age of ideology is over. On whose side, if anyone's, history is, no one can pretend to know. No one can say that history is on our side, and no one can enroll the Universe as a Whole into any political party. We can act to realize as far as we may our own, human values, but we do so without the knowledge that our embodiments and realizations are elected to withstand all time. The age of religious wars was followed by a time in which cosmopolitanism and the rational spirit were admired of men. There was an aspiration to rise above tribalism and national ethnocentrism to be a "citizen of the world." Those hopes of the eighteenth century foundered, but perhaps they will be renewed. When ideologies recede, humanity may discover for itself a common language and common values. When ideologies recede, it will be the ebb-tide of human hatreds, and the energies of men, disenthralled from conflict and suppression, will know new horizons of happiness and achievement.

And, suppose it were true that human hopes will be wrecked, that the dreams of radical reform will never live but on paper, suppose it were true that humankind lacks the resources for self-liberation. Would wisdom then dictate that we should retreat into ourselves? Is social action wise only when it has the warrant of success? Is there a basic imperative that one be always on the winning side?

There is a passage in Silone's great novel, *The Seed Beneath the Snow,* when Pietro Spina, wandering revolutionary, hiding in a hut with a donkey and a half-wit, is queried by a peasant friend:

"Pietro, don't you think that human society will always be ruled by some sort of oligarchy; that there will always be unfairness and oppression?"

"No, I don't believe so, Severi. And even so, what does it matter? We shall always be on the side of the poor."

Men's values in the end need make no obeisance to power and success. If the universe finally defeats human aspirations, it still remains true that the effort to realize them brings life to its fullest and most intense liberation. William James once spoke of "the potential social self" which lives as an ideal in human action: ". . . it may be represented as barely possible. I may not hope for its realization during my lifetime. . . . Yet still the emotion that beckons me on is indubitably the pursuit of an ideal social self. . . ."[6] This "ideal social self" consists of the affectional impulses of men, which have survived their dark oppressive surroundings, and which are looking for some way to the light of knowledge and human friendship. When social groups are dominated by hatred, when actual societies and persons have abandoned humane values, one's social feelings are directed towards man as he might be, a kingdom not of the present, but a kingdom which might be of this world. And if this hope founders, it will have given to life those moments which were free of anger and hatred, the moments which brought the fulness of joy which only love can bring.

References

1. Cf., Benedict, Ruth: *Patterns of Culture.* Boston, Houghton, 1934, p. 5, 22, 24, 37, 46-47, 52.
2. Cf., Benedict, Ruth: *Op. cit.,* p. 226, 247-248.
3. Mead, Margaret: The comparative study of culture and the purposive cultivation of democratic values, in *Science, Philosophy and Religion: Second Symposium,* edited by Lyman Bryson and Louis Finkelstein. New York, Harper, 1942, p. 57-58. Mead, Margaret: *Coming of Age in Samoa.* New York, W. Morrow, 1928, p. 212-213.
4. Ruth Benedict indeed held that all the laws of individual psychology would not explain the facts of cultural diversity. Cf., Benedict, Ruth: *Op. cit.,* p. 231.
5. Hitler, Adolf: *Mein Kampf.* New York, Reynal (Harcourt), 1941, p. 582-583, 84.
6. James, William: *The Principles of Psychology,* Vol. I. New York, Holt, 1890, p. 315.

INDEX

This Book

PSYCHOANALYSIS AND ETHICS

By

LEWIS SAMUEL FEUER

was set and printed by The Ovid Bell Press, Inc., of Fulton, Missouri. It was bound by The Becktold Company of St. Louis, Missouri. The page trim size is 5½ x 8½ inches. The type page is 23 x 39 picas. The type face is Baskerville, set 11 point on 13 point. The text paper is 70-pound Carfax eggshell. The cover is Roxite LS Vellum, 5175, 11-M, Two-tone Black.

With **THOMAS BOOKS** *careful attention is given to all details of manufacturing and design. It is the Publisher's desire to present books that are satisfactory as to their physical qualities and artistic possibilities and appropriate for their particular use.* **THOMAS BOOKS** *will be true to those laws of quality that assure a good name and good will.*

Date Due

JY 22 '68 APR 20 1970			
MY 5 '69			
MY 19 '69			
MAY 19			
MR 19 70			
MAR 23			
AP 6 '70			
APR 6			
AP 20 '70			
APR 6			
JY 15 76			
JY 14 '76			
MY 10 '77			
MY 3 '77			